BRAIN TINGLES

The Secret to Triggering
Autonomous Sensory Meridian Response
for Improved Sleep, Stress Relief,
and Head-to-Toe Euphoria

CRAIG RICHARD, PhD, Founder of ASMRUniversity.com
With a Foreword by Melinda Lauw, Artist and Cocreator of Whisperlodge

Adams Media
New York London Toronto Sydney New Delhi

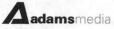

Adams Media
An Imprint of Simon & Schuster, Inc.
57 Littlefield Street
Avon, Massachusetts 02322

First Adams Media trade paperback edition September 2018

ADAMS MEDIA and colophon are trademarks of Simon & Schuster.

For information about special discounts for bulk purchases, please contact Simon & Schuster Special Sales at 1-866-506-1949 or business@simonandschuster.com.

The Simon & Schuster Speakers Bureau can bring authors to your live event. For more information or to book an event contact the Simon & Schuster Speakers Bureau at 1-866-248-3049 or visit our website at www.simonspeakers.com.

Interior design by Heather McKiel

Manufactured in the United States of America

10 9 8 7 6 5 4 3 2 1

Library of Congress Cataloging-in-Publication Data
Richard, Craig, author.
Brain tingles / Craig Richard, PhD, founder of ASMRUniversity.com; foreword by Melinda Lauw.
Avon, Massachusetts: Adams Media, 2018.
Includes bibliographical references and index.
LCCN 2018015132 | ISBN 9781507207628 (pb) | ISBN 9781507207635 (ebook)
Subjects: LCSH: ASMR (Intersensory effect) | Senses and sensation. | Sensory stimulation.
Classification: LCC BF233 .R496 2018 | DDC 152.1/8--dc23
LC record available at https://lccn.loc.gov/2018015132

ISBN 978-1-5072-0762-8
ISBN 978-1-5072-0763-5 (ebook)

CONTENTS

FOREWORD

My ASMR journey started in childhood. I remember feeling the tingles from the most random stimuli, like watching my teacher draw or getting a haircut. In my early teens, I constantly watched online videos that stimulated my ASMR. Then, I never really talked about my obsession because I did not know how to. In fact, I felt rather embarrassed about it.

I only learned about ASMR by chance, via a *YouTube* comment during one of my video-watching sessions. Suddenly, this thing had a name. I was not alone. ASMR is real and it is celebrated; as self-care, relief, relaxation, and pleasure.

Today, I have found myself at the forefront of the practice of ASMR. I am the cocreator of Whisperlodge, a live ASMR immersive experience that has toured New York, San Francisco, and Los Angeles. I am also the practitioner behind Whispers On Demand, a customizable live ASMR service. Trained as an artist, I started exploring live ASMR as an art project. Nobody had tried it at the time, so my friends and I did!

After over two years of performing live ASMR with people across America, I have learned that there is an innate joy when someone in your presence pays attention—to a thing, to a person, or to a specific sound or texture. Whether you wish to stimulate ASMR in another individual, or wish to simply receive it, the intention to be quiet and present in the moment is powerful enough to elicit a positive effect.

Craig's deep understanding of ASMR has allowed him to jump ahead of many lessons that I had to learn through trial and error. ASMR is a complicated and beautiful phenomenon, typically experienced individually. Practicing ASMR in person, however, takes it to a different level with new challenges. Live ASMR is relational and spatial, requiring considerations for consent, physical interaction, personal preferences, and visual aesthetics.

This book succeeds in distilling these challenges into a simple guide. Craig has spent years studying ASMR. His website, ASMRUniversity.com, is a valuable resource to the ASMR community, containing articles, research studies, and interviews, which have helped to articulate and legitimize ASMR. I found lots of Craig's recommendations to be congruent with my own practice, and I believe this book will be helpful to anyone interested in trying ASMR, whether it is for the camera, for friends, for clients, or for yourself.

ASMR is but one of the infinite number of sensations that we experience as humans. In many ways, this is about language. When we can name something, we are then able to share it and form community around it. The possibility for more of these idiosyncratic sensations to be named and explored is fascinating. I encourage you to experience life through your whole body, to be aware of how you uniquely perceive your world, and to maybe, give ASMR a shot!

—Melinda Lauw

INTRODUCTION

Do you get relaxed when someone plays with your hair? Does listening to someone whisper make you feel all calm and sleepy? Do you get tingles if someone lightly draws letters on your back with their finger?

These are all examples of Autonomous Sensory Meridian Response (ASMR), or, more informally, "brain tingles." This enjoyable, relaxing sensation can be a way to calm down, de-stress, and improve your mood. ASMR has recently become more well known because of its powerful ability to bring mindful relaxation to our busy modern world. Online ASMR videos with millions of views, ASMR-inspired commercials, celebrity ASMR videos, and even appearances in popular films like 2017's *Battle of the Sexes* have all helped put ASMR in the limelight.

Many people first experience ASMR by accident. Hairdressers, along with soothing teachers, reassuring clinicians, and your grandmother, aren't trying to induce brain tingles—it just happens through their caring, gentle mannerisms. If you've enjoyed the brain tingles you felt unintentionally, it's natural to want to seek them out. Luckily, there is a real treasure trove of ASMR triggering videos carefully and purposely created by ASMR artists for *YouTube*. There are also online videos that unintentionally trigger

ASMR in many viewers, like the popular TV show featuring Bob Ross painting.

But one of the most powerful ways to experience ASMR may be to have another person in your presence stimulate it. If you want to learn the art of stimulating ASMR on another person, you've come to the right place—this book will give you valuable insight on how to perform person-to-person ASMR. What you learn in this book could help you to soothe a distraught child, help a partner fall asleep more quickly, relax a friend after a stressful day, lift the mood of a family member, or perhaps add a new relaxation technique to your spa, wellness center, or counseling sessions.

The first part of the book will give you a concise but comprehensive understanding of ASMR. You'll learn what ASMR feels like, the general triggers for ASMR, the history of ASMR, why ASMR may exist, and most importantly, the potential physical and mental benefits of ASMR. Then we'll move on to selecting a comfortable partner, choosing and creating an ideal location, getting into a relaxing mind-set, and tailoring the ASMR session to best suit the other person.

The second part focuses on the main types of ASMR triggers, like gentle voices, light touches, soothing sounds, treasured objects, and focused activities. Each chapter will explain why that trigger type is relaxing and provide optimal techniques for you to use with that trigger type, along with a long list of tools and tips so you can create a deeply relaxing, enjoyable, and tingly ASMR experience for the other person. The third part of the book explains how to bring everything you've learned so far about ASMR and ASMR triggers to produce creative, immersive, and deeply relaxing role-plays.

Think of this book as a cookbook filled with the ingredients, recipes, and instructions for creating delightful ASMR. You'll learn some wonderful basic recipes, but over time you will develop your own style and techniques that won't be found in this or any other book. Evolve your style by being creative and requesting feedback from the other person. Good communication will enhance your ASMR techniques and sessions even further.

ASMR triggers may involve whispering, light touches, precise hand movements, and gentle sounds, but ASMR is mostly about genuinely caring for another person. If you bring that to every ASMR session, then you have the most important ingredient for bringing relaxation and comfort to those around you.

PART 1
UNDERSTANDING ASMR

Autonomous Sensory Meridian Response might sound complex, but the pleasant, refreshing sensations it provides may actually be one of the most basic human experiences. In this section, you'll discover exactly what brain tingles are, what triggers them, why they feel good, and some of the physical and mental benefits of experiencing them. After that, you'll learn background information about how to perform successful partner ASMR.

CHAPTER 1
WHAT IS ASMR?

ASMR DEFINED

ASMR stands for "Autonomous Sensory Meridian Response." That's a fancy term to describe that enjoyable and relaxing tingly feeling some people experience on their scalps, heads, and rest of their bodies from time to time. Although not everyone experiences it, many people across the globe—men and women of all ages and ethnicities—feel it. As word spreads online about ASMR, it's becoming a more and more popular way to relax.

In order to experience ASMR, something has to "trigger" the sensation. Some popular triggers for ASMR include having someone whisper softly to you, play gently with your hair, or open a package slowly in front of you. Triggers are a very personal preference—people are as picky, sensitive, and particular about their ASMR triggers as they are about their food or music preferences. Most people agree about the pleasant sensations that ASMR provides, which is why they turn to it for stress relief.

WHAT DOES ASMR FEEL LIKE?

You can feel ASMR in both physical and psychological ways, and different people experience the sensations differently.

PHYSICAL SENSATIONS OF ASMR

The most common physical manifestation of ASMR is the brain tingles. The tingling sensations are usually felt in the head, brain, or scalp but may be felt throughout other parts of the body too. Sometimes these sensations are described as sparkly or staticky.

Pause Point

Have you ever gotten the chills during a specific part of a song? It may happen when the music swells or when the vocalist sings something in a particular way. That special feeling is called *frisson.* Its physical manifestation is often called "the chills" or "goose-bumps." There is also a psychological or emotional aspect that is enjoyable but more difficult to describe. ASMR is similar to frisson because it also has a physical aspect and a psychological aspect, but the sensations during ASMR are somewhat different from those felt during frisson.

PSYCHOLOGICAL SENSATIONS OF ASMR

Brain tingles seem to be the most common signature of ASMR, but they may not be the most important. The deep enjoyment that ASMR brings people is probably actually more tied to the psychological and emotional sensations—most importantly, relaxation. In fact, ASMR can be so relaxing that many people utilize it to help them fall asleep. Several research studies have confirmed that relaxation is the most common psychological feeling during an ASMR experience, and it is the most common reason people watch ASMR videos. People also describe ASMR as calming, soothing, comforting, and enjoyable. These pleasant sensations are the root of ASMR's increasing popularity.

WHAT TRIGGERS ASMR?

"ASMR triggers" is the term for the interesting variety of things that can stimulate ASMR. These triggers can take the form of a voice, a sound, a touch, observing another person, or receiving attention from someone. A combination of several of these trigger types, weaved into a real or fictional situation, can be referred to as a scenario or role-play.

AUDIO TRIGGERS

The human voice works wonderfully as an audio trigger. Whispering has been reported by several research studies to be the most popular of all the ASMR triggers, but just talking in a relaxing voice is also one. Interestingly, it is how you speak that makes it a trigger, not what you actually say.

A huge variety of other sounds can also be audio triggers for ASMR:

- Crinkling paper or plastic
- Tapping different objects
- Scratching materials
- Squishing wet items
- Making sticky sounds with your fingers
- Creating mechanical sounds with devices like keyboards or scissors
- Chewing or drinking
- Performing actions like turning papers, opening jars, and playing with beads

We'll talk more about auditory triggers in Chapters 3 and 4.

TOUCH TRIGGERS

Touch-mediated ASMR is usually done in a light, gentle, and careful way. Many people like to have their skin traced—the lines in their palm, small marks on their skin, or the vessels on the surface of their arms. Hair and scalp touching or stroking, which can include braiding, weaving, twirling, brushing, or just gentle hair play, is also very popular. Soft makeup brushes used on the face, arms, or back can create exhilarating tingles as well. Touch triggers will be the focus of Chapters 5 and 6.

OBSERVATION TRIGGERS

Observation-based triggers are called this because they involve watching another person who is focused on an item or activity. Examples include the following:

- Watching someone sort through a collection of items, such as coins, stickers, CDs, cassettes, baseball cards, buttons, spools, pens, and even paper clips.
- Watching someone open a package, like a box received in the mail; unwrapping a product from its packaging; showing a purchase from a local store; and opening a gift.
- Watching someone perform a specific activity or task, like drawing, coloring, solving a jigsaw puzzle, applying makeup, having his or her hair brushed, using a calculator, demonstrating a device, or teaching a task or skill like how to play chess.

Pause Point

Perhaps the most famous observational trigger is Bob Ross, known for his relaxing style of landscape oil painting showcased on his TV series, *The Joy of Painting*. You can visit his official *YouTube* channel at www.youtube.com/channel/UCxcnsr1R5Ge_fbTu5ajt8DQ to watch episodes or clips.

Chapters 7 and 8 will go into a lot more depth about observation-based triggers.

SCENARIO TRIGGERS

Scenario-based triggers involve receiving attention, usually as a simulated situation called a *role-play*. Examples include pretending to get a haircut, getting an eye exam, or getting assistance from a teacher. These triggers can stimulate strong ASMR because the scenario fully immerses the person in a variety of triggers, including personal attention from someone with a caring disposition. Some popular scenarios include the following:

- Touch-based scenarios, such as cranial nerve exams, haircuts, and makeup applications.
- Hands-off scenarios, such as eye exams with an eye chart; a pharmacist consultation; interviewing for a job or loan; taking a survey; and being sketched, drawn, or painted.

Chapters 9 and 10 will offer tips, techniques, and lots of ideas for role-plays.

A BRIEF HISTORY OF ASMR

The discovery of ASMR is not a single moment; it is more of a journey of awareness and understanding. This journey is still in progress and far from complete. It is probably safe to say that right now there are more unknowns about ASMR than knowns.

THE SEED: AN ONLINE FORUM

On October 29, 2007, someone with the username okay-whatever51838 started a forum thread at SteadyHealth.com.

The title of the thread was "Weird sensation feels good." Okaywhatever51838's first post described pleasurable sensations he or she received when he or she was read to or someone drew on the palm of his or her hand. The first reply was from someone who mentioned that when people talked slowly to him or her, he or she felt a tingling in his or her head and a feeling like a head orgasm.

Pause Point

You can still visit this original forum thread to read the responses at www.steadyhealth.com/topics/weird-sensation-feels-good. This forum thread was probably the first place people shared links to individual videos for the stimulation of ASMR.

The forum thread kept getting more replies. Each reply was basically "Me too!" with a list of personal triggers and more questions. The thread grew to have hundreds of replies over the years. Several of the early participants in this forum thread went on to create the first ASMR discussion sites on *Facebook*, a community-focused ASMR blog (*The Unnamed Feeling* at http://theunnam3df33ling.blogspot.com/), and the first ASMR research website (the currently inactive www.asmr-research.org).

FIRST ASMR *YOUTUBE* CHANNEL

In early 2009, there were some "whisper videos" loosely scattered throughout *YouTube*. These videos were not created and posted with the intention of relaxing and soothing viewers; people were just whispering because they did not want to be heard by other people nearby, e.g., they were in a library, near a sleeping person, or conspiring on a reality TV show. Yet these whisper videos appealed greatly to a growing niche audience who deeply enjoyed and were relaxed by listening to videos of people whispering.

Those whispering videos inspired a young woman in Nottingham, England, to create a channel on *YouTube*. On March 26, 2009, she started posting videos of herself whispering and called her *YouTube* channel WhisperingLife (www.youtube.com/watch?v=IHtgPbfTgKc&t=1s). Over the following years, she uploaded more than 150 videos that were mostly whisper videos but also included some trigger sounds of keyboards, doodling, and magazines.

She is considered the first ASMR artist because she was the first person to create a *YouTube* channel that only contained videos of whispering or trigger sounds for the relaxation and enjoyment of the viewers. (She was not called an ASMR artist in 2009, though, because that term wasn't coined until 2010.)

BIRTH OF THE TERM "ASMR"

Jennifer Allen, a healthcare manager, was one of the early participants in the forum thread started by okaywhatever51838 in 2007. She then went on to make several important contributions to the ASMR community. She founded the ASMR *Facebook* group, the ASMR *Facebook* page, and the ASMR research website. She also made one other major contribution: she coined the term "Autonomous Sensory Meridian Response." Each word helps encapsulate the physical and psychological effects:

- The word *autonomous* acknowledges that these stimuli can be different for different people, including the ability of some people to stimulate ASMR in themselves.

- The word *sensory* refers to the input of stimuli like sights, sounds, and touches that can initiate ASMR.
- The word *meridian*, in this case meaning "greatest prosperity" or "splendor," is an acknowledgment that the response is deeply relaxing and enjoyable.
- The word *response* indicates that these stimuli initiate a specific effect.

Pause Point

Allen knew that ASMR, or "brain orgasms" as it was commonly called back then, was very difficult to describe and that people who felt it might feel awkward or confused talking about it. She thought about both these challenges while coming up with a name. As she explained in a 2016 interview with ASMRUniversity.com, "I knew with something as difficult to describe and as sensitive for people to open up about as ASMR that we would need something that objectively and definitively named the sensation. Using a 'clinical' word was the best option to improve how the burgeoning community would feel about using and telling others about the word."

ASMR'S RISE IN POPULARITY

The early online ASMR forums, *Facebook* groups, and *YouTube* channels united a previously scattered community of people who enjoyed practicing and sharing their experiences about brain tingles. From there, the relaxing power of ASMR began getting wider attention from mainstream media. A memorable radio moment happened for ASMR in March 2013, when NPR broadcast a story about ASMR titled "A Tribe Called Rest" for the *This American Life* audio program (you can hear the program at www.thisamericanlife.org/491/tribes). The following year ASMR had a memorable TV moment when actress Molly Shannon spoke excitedly about ASMR as a guest on *Conan* in May 2014 (you can watch the clip at www.youtube.com /watch?v=VjHIfei0WZE).

Since then, ASMR has continued to spread into many different facets of culture. For example, you can find it in varied types of musical outlets, from rap songs to operas. Recent movies, live comedy, and performance art have included scenes meant to stimulate ASMR. Check out a list of ASMR-inspired art here: https://asmruniversity.com/art-of-asmr-description-examples/. Many well-known celebrities have professed their interest in ASMR, and some have even tried their hands at creating ASMR triggers:

- Actor Ashton Kutcher said this about ASMR on his *Facebook* page: "Mind blown (insert sound effect of mind exploding... In a good way)": www.facebook.com/Ashton/ posts/10152797394077820
- Actress Gal Gadot, who starred in the *Wonder Woman* movie, appears in a short ASMR video that includes whispering, opening up a snack bag, eating chocolate, and writing with a pencil: www.youtube.com/watch?v=HOfsCvdfyzk
- Actress Kate Hudson created some intentional ASMR triggers in a video by whispering, twirling water in a mug, rustling fabrics, scratching on a belt, and creating scissor sounds: www.youtube.com/watch?v=Vgs-h53tg8U
- Actresses Sadie Sink, Dakota Fanning, Elle Fanning, Julia Garner, and Chloë Sevigny created a short and mysterious holiday video filled with ASMR triggering whispers: www.youtube.com/watch?v=boRH4Xgpe4s

Companies have also incorporated the happy and relaxed feelings that ASMR creates in their commercials and marketing messages. Dove, Pepsi, KFC, Ritz, IKEA, Toyota, Sony, and Glenmorangie whiskey have all created ASMR-inspired commercials. IKEA's advertisement was more than twenty-five minutes long and can be found on *YouTube* with the title, "'Oddly IKEA': IKEA ASMR": www.youtube.com/watch?v=uLFaj3Z_tWw.

Clearly, ASMR appeals to a lot of people—and those numbers are growing every day. But why exactly do these brain tingles feel so good? Turns out, there might be an evolutionary reason rooted in our brain chemicals.

BIOLOGICAL ORIGINS OF ASMR

ASMR has been widely reported by individuals all across the globe. This strongly suggests it is a biological response. Almost all our biological functions and reactions, no matter how peculiar, somehow benefit us. The benefit usually is related to helping us prevent or recover from an illness or other unhealthy state. Being able to soothe and relax a crying infant or anyone we care for will reduce their stress hormones and therefore boost their health.

> **"I remember ASMR from a very early age— from my mum stroking my hair so I could sleep on the train, to my nana's soft voice."**
>
> —Imperfect ASMR, *YouTube* artist, UK

Perhaps the most important trait of all ASMR triggers is that they make you feel relaxed. Imagine the disposition of your favorite ASMR artist or any individuals who give you tingles. Chances are they speak gently, have a caring tone to their voices, and have genuine and sincere personalities. Their behavior and character make you feel safe.

If that person is creating ASMR trigger sounds, even the sounds seem safe. Trigger sounds tend to be repetitive, methodical, gentle, at a steady pace, and at low and/or steady volume. If the person started creating sounds that were loud, frenetic, and unpredictable, then you would find the sounds and the person creating those sounds disturbing, threatening, and not relaxing.

If we are experiencing gentle sounds, touches, and behaviors around us, our brains convert those signals into chemicals that make us feel relaxed and safe.

THE ROLE OF OXYTOCIN IN ASMR

A single brain chemical, oxytocin, has been dubbed "the trust hormone" or "the love hormone" because it is produced when people trust and care for each other. This brain chemical has been shown to increase when children and parents interact, when romantic partners cuddle, when friends spend time together, and even when dog owners pet their dogs. Many ASMR triggers are directly related to these same caring interactions. From birth to adulthood, humans tend to bond with individuals (including parents, family members, best friends, and romantic partners) who perform these actions because their behaviors seem trustworthy.

> **"I think ASMR helps people bond with others. I tend to feel close to or gravitate toward people who trigger ASMR in me. I also find myself looking forward to situations where I think it will happen, such as haircuts, eye exams, or interactive theater."**
>
> —Juliet, 32, female, USA

OXYTOCIN AND GIVING CARE

Many moments that trigger ASMR are quite similar to a parent watching over a focused child. ASMR is often triggered by watching someone color, draw, use a device, handle a bunch of items, or open a package. Observing these activities may increase the release of oxytocin, along with the feelings of being focused, relaxed, and perhaps even sleepy.

To understand this connection, it helps to know a little more about the role of oxytocin in parental care. Parents, especially mothers, produce high levels of oxytocin while caring for their children. The oxytocin actually stimulates the parents to show more interest and focused care toward their children while also producing feelings of relaxation. The relaxing feelings induced by the oxytocin may be because the child is safe and occupied so the parent doesn't need to be on high alert. In fact, an engaged child might have evolved as a stimulus to induce relaxation and perhaps even sleepiness because it might be a safer time for a parent to fall asleep than when the child requires direct care.

Pause Point

Studies have shown that oxytocin release makes people feel calmer and happier while decreasing their levels of fear and stress. Because of its role in relaxation and happiness, oxytocin has even been proposed as a medical treatment for anxiety, depression, and other disorders.

OXYTOCIN AND RECEIVING CARE

On the flip side, many ASMR triggers are similar to receiving personal attention from parents, family members, friends, partners, therapists, and clinicians. Examples of these triggers include someone speaking to you gently, looking at you in a caring way, touching you lightly, reading to you, sharing a story with you, tracing your palm, brushing your hair, and giving you a cranial nerve exam.

Pause Point

What about people who don't experience ASMR? They probably actually are experiencing it, but their feelings of relaxation are subtler. This may be related to how their bodies produce or react to oxytocin. Perhaps ASMR-sensitive individuals produce higher than average amounts of oxytocin in response to triggers. Another possibility is that they produce average amounts of oxytocin but their receptors to it are more sensitive or numerous than those in other people.

Being the recipient of these specific behaviors may stimulate the release of oxytocin and therefore the feeling of relaxation. This is the key to how oxytocin bonds parents and infants. Picking up a fussy baby is soothing to the parent and to the infant. The tricky part is that infants need to be born with some built-in system that allows them to figure out if the creature who just approached them is going to be helpful or harmful. It is likely that they will relax if the other person is speaking softly or whispering, using a loving tone, gazing at them in a caring way, touching them lightly on their hands or skin, playing with their hair, slowly moving his or her hands in front of them, and perhaps even repeating specific words or sounds.

Pause Point

Parental care–type behaviors don't just soothe infants; they also soothe children and adults. In terms of human survival, the behaviors are simply communicating that the other person is nonthreatening and that he or she cares about you. Though you're not a cave person whose life is being threatened, there are times in modern life when you need to trust certain strangers in situations in which you are vulnerable. Examples include a visit with a masseuse, a therapist, a clinician, or a scissor-wielding hairdresser. Their expertise, professionalism, caring natures, and gentle personalities seem to be the core traits of an ASMR-stimulating disposition.

OTHER BRAIN CHEMICALS

Could other brain chemicals be responsible for the sensations and potential benefits of ASMR? Yes. Research has shown that when parents soothe infants, a teacher comforts a sad child, or lovers cuddle on the couch, a brain cocktail of several chemicals is released:

- **Endorphins** are known for inducing relaxation, sleepiness, and pleasure and reducing pain.
- **Dopamine** provides a powerful stimulus for desire and focus.
- **Serotonin** is known for increasing contentment, satisfaction, and happiness.
- **GABA** is a strong stimulator of relaxation and sleepiness.
- **Melatonin** plays an important role in the initiation and quality of sleep.

It is likely that all these chemicals work together to contribute to the effects of ASMR.

BENEFITS OF ASMR

The real magic of ASMR is the wonderful feelings it can produce. People report that ASMR helps them feel relaxed, deal with stress, fall asleep more easily, and feel happier. Because the ASMR phenomenon is in its infancy, not a lot of clinical research studies have been devoted to how and why it works and its potential benefits. As a result, most information available on ASMR benefits comes from ASMR participants who have completed surveys about their experiences. If you've enjoyed ASMR triggers before, you've likely felt some of these benefits. If you're new to ASMR, the following are some of the physical and psychological benefits you might experience.

Pause Point

Many studies need to occur before the health benefits of ASMR can be scientifically and clinically proven. If you are struggling with a health condition, make sure to discuss it with your clinician. Ask your doctor if ASMR might be used to complement whatever he or she recommended as a treatment.

RELAXATION

Perhaps the most popular benefit of ASMR is how relaxed people feel when they experience it. After a busy day, the soothing tones and gentle touches of ASMR triggers could help loosen the tension in your shoulders and calm your racing thoughts.

> **"Relaxing doesn't have to be a solution to a problem; it can be enjoyed like a glass of wine. ASMR is helpful for any time relaxation is desired."**
>
> —Brandon, 32, male, USA

People of all ages find ASMR relaxing. For example, children who are frustrated or upset might benefit from ten minutes of gentle hair play or light brushing on their arms.

> **"I have seen the benefits of ASMR on children with special-needs. It helps calm and relax them but also make them feel happy in some way."**
>
> —CoconutsWhisper, *YouTube* artist, UK

DECREASED STRESS AND ANXIETY

Stress, at one time or another, is a significant challenge for most people. It is not just a bad feeling; very real health problems can result from stress, especially chronic stress. Chronic stress can cause problems with digestion, sleep, and reproduction and can worsen issues like heart disease, hypertension, diabetes, depression, infections, and other mental and physical illnesses. If extreme stress becomes detrimental to a person's health, job, relationships, goals, or lifestyle, he or she may be diagnosed with an anxiety disorder.

> **"ASMR helps me calm down when I am on the verge of a panic attack. It also helps to draw me out of a 'low moment' induced by my bipolar."**
>
> —Erin, 27, female, USA

Experiencing ASMR could therefore be a helpful reprieve after a mentally or physically exhausting day. Having a friend braid your hair or asking your partner to ramble softly about his or her day while lightly touching your arm could help bring you back to a calm and happy place.

> "I was experiencing ASMR as a child before
> I knew it had a name. It relaxed me more
> accurately than anything else. I have ADHD and
> find it hard to slow down mentally. This causes
> a lot of anxiety. ASMR is one of the few
> things I can count on to consistently
> calm me."

—Kim, 39, female, Canada

REDUCED SLEEPLESSNESS AND INSOMNIA

Getting enough sleep is a common challenge for many people. There are many reasons for modern sleep debt—the lure and light of electronic devices in bed, the challenges at work, the constant deadlines of school, and all of our other daily responsibilities and worries are usually at the top of the list.

> "ASMR absolutely helps me to relax and
> de-stress. I use it every night before bed
> to help me relax and then sleep."

—Suz, 50, female, USA

Feeling drowsy during the day is only one of the problems that can arise. A lack of quality sleep can result in impaired learning and memory and increased difficulties with anxiety and depression, and it can also worsen heart problems, diabetes, infections, breathing difficulties, and obesity. If inadequate sleep begins causing problems with someone's health, job, relationships, goals, or lifestyle, a doctor might diagnose insomnia. Experiencing ASMR right before bed, or perhaps even earlier in the day, could help with a more restful night of sleep.

MINIMIZED SADNESS AND DEPRESSION

Pretty much everyone experiences sad moods from time to time, but persistent sadness is more devastating and can result in eating disorders, altered libido, aggression, social withdrawal, lack of self-care, low self-esteem, and other problems. If a persistent low mood affects someone's health, job, relationships, goals, or lifestyle in detrimental ways, a doctor might diagnose depression, which may be treated with medication or another type of therapy.

ASMR may help buffer moments of sadness. A 2015 study published in *PeerJ* showed that those at high risk for depression reported that watching ASMR videos improved their mood. Some of your favorite ASMR triggers could help to lift your mood.

IMPROVED OVERALL WELL-BEING

In addition to the specific benefits, experiencing ASMR can simply help improve your well-being. Similar to going to a yoga class, visiting a spa, or watching your favorite TV program, having an ASMR session with another person can give you a personalized and relaxing time to look forward to. ASMR can complement any calming or meditative practice you might already enjoy—helping you to refocus and center yourself if you feel overwhelmed and scattered.

> **"I believe we've only scratched the surface of the potential benefits of not only identifying but stimulating ASMR in instances of depression, anxiety, PTSD, insomnia, etc. Knowing how utilizing ASMR so positively affects me, why wouldn't I want to seek it out for fostering overall well-being?"**
>
> —Karen Schweiger, CuddleInYourArms.com, USA

CHAPTER 2
PREPARING FOR ASMR

ASMR is easy to incorporate into your daily life, either alone or with a partner. If you're alone, you can watch online videos that match your preferences or even try out some triggers, like using a scalp massaging device on yourself. At some point, though, you are probably going to wonder what it would be like if someone stimulated your ASMR directly, and if you could do the same for them.

However, assuming anyone who can whisper can stimulate ASMR is like assuming anyone with a massage table gives a great massage. It is a good start, but there are many other factors. You'll need to know the best way to prepare a session that's comfortable and relaxing for both of you. This chapter will help you create soothing and enjoyable ASMR sessions.

WHEN IS ASMR USEFUL?

Thanks to its ability to relax and soothe, there are countless times when ASMR might help you, a friend, or a loved one. An ASMR session—whether solitary or partner-based, online or offline, formal or informal, long or short—could be beneficial in common situations like these:

- Helping a restless child fall asleep
- Relaxing a partner while sitting on the couch
- Unwinding a loved one after a busy work day
- Calming someone down before a big presentation or interview
- Soothing a friend having relationship troubles
- Helping a family member remain calm on an airplane
- Recentering someone overwhelmed by responsibilities
- Inducing tingles in a friend curious about ASMR

The more familiar you become with ASMR, the more instances you'll likely find to help someone you know to feel more relaxed. You may also be interested in providing ASMR as a service to people you may not know well. There are many people who may be more comfortable paying for an ASMR session from a skilled individual rather than asking someone they know well.

> **"As a mental health therapist who sometimes uses mindfulness in her practice, I wonder about incorporating it into sessions with clients. I love the idea of using ASMR to facilitate bonding between a parent and child who have been having relationship difficulties."**
>
> —Kristina, 44, female, USA

ENJOYING ASMR ALONE

Watching ASMR videos is perhaps the most common way of experiencing solitary ASMR. The major advantages of videos for experiencing ASMR are the twenty-four-hour access, the huge variety of content, and the no-cost access. Although solitary ASMR sounds like a negative term, the fact that you do it alone is also a major reason it works so well. You don't need to worry about scheduling a session or inconveniencing another person or wonder what the content creator might be thinking about you, and most importantly, you never feel unsafe. These advantages of ASMR videos will make them a permanent and valuable way to experience ASMR.

> ## "A lot of people with anxiety don't like people to be too close to them. Some may find in-person ASMR too intense."
>
> —Amanda, WhisperSparkles ASMR, *YouTube* artist, UK

Beyond watching online videos, some people report being able to stimulate their own ASMR. (Some people even say it is the only way they can experience ASMR.) It's not always easy, in the same way that it is difficult to tickle yourself, but it works for some people. Being in a calm mind-set and a relaxing environment can be helpful. Knowing your personal preferences and experimenting via trial and error are two good ways to see if you may be able to experience solitary ASMR.

Every person is different, but here are some examples of ASMR triggers that sometimes work for self-stimulation:

- Concentrating on any general aspect or specific part of yourself
- Using a scalp massager or slightly touching your scalp with your fingers
- Brushing or playing with your hair
- Stroking or rubbing your eyebrows

- Thinking about doing any of the previous triggers, or any ASMR trigger, to yourself
- Thinking about someone else stimulating you with an ASMR trigger

Experiencing solitary ASMR may help you to understand your own ASMR better, and even help you to be more comfortable experiencing partner-based ASMR.

SOLITARY VERSUS PARTNER ASMR

While many people enjoy watching videos or practicing solitary ASMR, having someone directly stimulate your ASMR can be a different experience. You might want to feel the personalized touch of someone else playing with your hair or using soft brushes on you. You might want tingles that can arise from close personal attention like having someone next to you whisper in your ears. Perhaps you have discovered that videos don't stimulate your ASMR, or you are considering starting a walk-in ASMR service. Or, maybe you are just an adventurous spirit and experiencing ASMR with another individual sounds fun and interesting to you. If any of these reasons resonate with you, then you might want to try partner ASMR.

The rest of this chapter will walk you through important considerations you should think about before your first partner ASMR session. Still, keep your solitary practices in mind because the understanding and insights you get about partner ASMR may also help you enjoy solitary ASMR even more, and vice versa.

WHAT IS PARTNER ASMR?

Let's begin with a clarification of what partner ASMR means. Partner ASMR is just a shorter way of saying, "Two people get together in real life with the understanding that one person is going to stimulate ASMR in the other person." If you feel ASMR at the hairdresser or with a clinician, that is not partner ASMR because the person was not intending to stimulate your ASMR. The moment when partner ASMR occurs is called an ASMR session.

WHO CAN PARTICIPATE?

You could offer an ASMR session to someone you already know well, like a friend, a family member, or a romantic partner. If you have children, family, or friends, then you are surrounded by people who could probably benefit from a special relaxation session at times. ASMR can be an intimate sensation, so you may prefer to give ASMR to, or receive ASMR from, someone you don't know well.

> **"Everything about a live, person-to-person ASMR session sounds appealing to me! My ideal location to experience an ASMR live session would have to be in a spa-type setting. I could pick my trigger, meet someone in the room, we would do a meet and greet beforehand so I don't feel completely awkward, and then there could be a choice of sounds in the background."**
>
> —Hannah Carter, 30, female, USA

ASMR sessions can also be offered as a service, similar to paying a masseuse, a relaxation coach, or a private yoga instructor. Many people may find this appealing because they may want a more professional-type session with an experienced practitioner of ASMR triggers. ASMR sessions can be incorporated into spas or wellness centers or as independent services like Whisperlodge.

ASMR CLASSES

Although ASMR probably works best one on one, you might want to consider offering ASMR classes if you feel others may feel more comfortable experiencing ASMR in a group setting. ASMR classes could be held at local gyms, health studios, fitness centers, or any location that already offers yoga, Pilates, group meditation, progressive muscle relaxation, stress management, or breathing exercise classes.

An ASMR class could be structured like a yoga class but would have some additional challenges. The participants may need to wear wireless headsets to hear the instructor's microphone-assisted whispers, soft voice, and trigger sounds. Light touch could be incorporated by having participants partner up and then having the instructor guide them through specific light-touch activities, like touching each other's backs.

WORKING WITH A PARTNER

Selecting the other person for an ASMR session is perhaps the most important consideration. In essence, both individuals are partners in the ASMR session. Selecting the right partner may actually be key to being able to induce tingles.

"I imagine that an ASMR practitioner would be empathic, kind, warm, nonjudgmental, and open."

—Karissa, 28, female, USA

ASMR seems to be a sensation that mostly occurs in the presence of individuals who trust each other. It would be unlikely for a sketchy-looking stranger on the street to be able to stimulate ASMR in you. Most people report experiencing ASMR from one or more of the following:

- A loving family member
- A close friend
- A romantic partner
- A caring teacher
- A health professional
- A spa or hair salon employee

The origin of ASMR may be rooted in the ability to form a safe and caring connection with the person you're working with. As discussed in Chapter 1, the relaxing sensation of ASMR may be your brain's way of telling you that you are safe and in good hands.

Regardless of the evolutionary backstory of ASMR, there are more obvious reasons to select your ASMR partner carefully. Most ASMR sessions are going to involve two individuals in a private setting in close proximity and may include light touching.

Pause Point

Even if you're very curious to try ASMR, be sure to use good judgment about whom you try it with. Only schedule ASMR sessions with trusted professionals or individuals you know well in locations where you feel comfortable. As a best practice, always let friends and family members know where you are and who you are with.

WORKING WITH SOMEONE YOU KNOW

If you have a close friend or family member who also enjoys ASMR, it might be easy for you to partner up with that person. You two can dive right into each person's individual likes and what times would be mutually agreeable.

Pause Point

Even if you know a person well, he or she is not necessarily a good ASMR partner. A person's mood, intention, voice, personality, and technique can all affect the overall ASMR experience. There's also the intangible connection you two may or may not have—whether or not you two "click" as ASMR partners even if you get along great in other ways.

If you want to ask a close friend or family member to try ASMR with you but that person doesn't know about it, you might want to give him or her a little background on ASMR when you ask. Show or loan the other person this book, send a link to a useful website or article about ASMR, and discuss ASMR with him or her. Give your potential partner some time to learn about ASMR, then follow up with a discussion and invitation to try an ASMR session.

SETTING UP AN ASMR SESSION

Once you know who you'll be working with, it's time to think about how you'd like the session to be arranged. Even if you want to keep things simple and casual, it helps to put in some thought ahead of time to so you can maximize your relaxation and enjoyment and avoid potential hiccups.

"Performing ASMR is a combination of being your authentic self and also being a sensual, dreamy version of yourself. Live ASMR provides real closeness. You're sharing a curated moment of intimacy and sensory pleasure with a real human giving you their undivided attention, and that's a potent scenario. I've found that the best live ASMR guides are soft, nurturing, knowledgeable about ASMR culture, and comfortable with intimacy."

—Andrew Hoepfner, cocreator of Whisperlodge, USA

EXPECTATIONS

First off—it's important to have realistic expectations. The fact is that not everyone can experience ASMR, and not everyone can stimulate ASMR in you. This can add a large and frustrating challenge to an ASMR session.

As difficult as it is, especially if you are really looking forward to trying ASMR, don't expect every ASMR session to be a tingle fest. Selecting the right ASMR trigger, creating the optimal environment, and having a comforting technique and disposition can all affect ASMR. Usually, though, the first thought someone has if he or she doesn't feel ASMR right away is that he or she must not experience it. This could be true, but it might not be.

If someone didn't like one particular food choice on a buffet table, then he or she probably shouldn't conclude that he or she doesn't like *any* of the food in the buffet. Similarly, someone can't conclude he or she doesn't experience ASMR after only trying a few triggers. He or she needs to try different triggers in different environments with different people. ASMR trigger preferences are highly subjective and can require a trial-and-error process. Patience is one of the most important things to bring to an ASMR session.

It will take a lot of patience and experimentation before you can start believing that someone doesn't experience ASMR. After an appropriate number of attempts without ASMR, you may come to the obvious conclusion. Therefore, it is important to never guarantee or expect that every person will experience ASMR. On the other hand, there is also opportunity for a great discovery. One of the most joyous moments you may have is when you discover that you or the other person actually does experience ASMR.

> **"Because of the strong sense of wellness when experiencing ASMR, I imagine helping another person enjoy it could be the basis of very strong emotions of fondness and appreciation toward each other."**
>
> —Monika, 22, female, Norway

It is also important to not get too fixated on ASMR as the only goal. Your goal is to provide a relaxing and enjoyable experience for the other person. Many people report that they enjoy ASMR videos and find them relaxing even though they don't believe they experience ASMR. In a similar manner, you may greatly enjoy a song, even though it does not give you those deep chills and frisson.

So keep trying—with the goal of relaxation and the possible result of ASMR. Knowing ahead of time that things might not initially work out can keep both parties motivated to try again with a different trigger or partner. The good news is that there are several things both parties can focus on ahead of time to give the session the best chance of success, such as location, specific triggers, and personal preferences.

LOCATION

A major consideration for any ASMR session is creating a relaxing and comfortable environment. Setting up a massage table in the middle of a rock concert probably won't result in the best massage. An ideal environment for a massage usually involves a dimly lit room, a warm temperature, and a quiet space. Similarly, you want all the factors of the environment of your ASMR session to enhance, not inhibit, the ability to experience ASMR.

A 2015 research study by Barratt and Davis at Swansea University reported that 52 percent of the participants required specific conditions to achieve ASMR. Notice that these individuals said they "required," and didn't just prefer, specific conditions. For many people, an appropriate location may be just as important to a successful ASMR session as the list of ASMR triggers and a good partner.

> **"The possibility of a personalized ASMR experience interests me. If it's in the city, it needs to be soundproof and private. In the countryside, open windows and ambient nature sounds would be acceptable if the weather is appropriate. The decor doesn't have to be minimalist but should at least be cozy, and no fluorescent lights! Basically nothing that stands out enough to distract you or to make your mind wander."**
>
> —Kim, 39, female, Canada

Most ASMR enthusiasts would prefer a clean, quiet, and relaxed location, so start by selecting a space that is free of other people and away from street noise. Remove or turn off anything in the space that may detract from a relaxing moment. Turn off

TVs, silence electronic devices, and scoot pets out. A 2017 study by Barratt, Spence, and Davis published in *PeerJ* reported that music may inhibit strong ASMR tingles, so keep the music off unless it is requested. You can enhance the relaxing and comforting atmosphere by adding candles or dimmed lights, laying rugs over hard floors, and draping silk scarves over furniture.

> **"An ASMR center would be the place of my dreams. You would have the possibility to sit or to lie down. I think that you should personalize an ASMR session before starting and ask to the listener which triggers he likes the most."**
>
> —Paris ASMR, *YouTube* artist, France

If possible, also try to create a comfortable temperature. If the area is too hot or too cold, then that can make it harder to experience ASMR. If the temperature is not appropriate, each person's body will become less relaxed and more focused on trying to get cooler or hotter. A room that is too cool may also result in cold hands and fingers, which will also be inhibitive to stimulating ASMR.

> **"For me, room temperature is a primary factor in whether I can experience ASMR. Also somewhere private as it wouldn't happen for me in a crowded place or if I was being watched."**
>
> —WhisperHub, *YouTube* artist, UK

SCHEDULING

Some times of the day may be more optimal for ASMR than other times. Again, this is a very individual choice that depends on the type of trigger you or your partner likes, whether you're doing it alone or with a partner, and what your daily schedule looks like.

Bedtime

The 2015 Swansea University research study reported that 81 percent of participants watched ASMR videos before sleeping. This is an ideal time and place for doing ASMR alone because you're in a safe and comfortable place, reclined, and your mind is starting to drift off into a relaxing and sleep-ready state. Bedtime would also be the perfect time for anyone trying an ASMR session as part of a sleepover with friends or to wind down with a romantic partner. However, this setting is not going to be the ideal time and place for other types of ASMR sessions.

Midafternoon

Midafternoon is another good time for ASMR stimulation. Human biology and behavior have certain patterns throughout a day, often referred to as circadian rhythms. One aspect of our daily rhythms is how sleepy we feel, which, as most of us know, does *not* just occur at bedtime. The other time of day when we often feel a sleepy slump is in the midafternoon, between 2:00 p.m. and 4:00 p.m. For that reason, it might be an ideal time for an ASMR session if it fits into your daily schedule.

Pause Point

Knowing the effect of food on relaxation might also help you with the timing of ASMR sessions. For example, ASMR sessions may work better after meals than before meals when hunger and alertness might hinder tingles. Caffeine and nicotine are additional concerns because they also stimulate alertness. Try to avoid smoking, coffee, and other caffeine-containing drinks before an ASMR session.

You may have heard that this midafternoon slump is due to eating lunch, but this is not entirely true. People who don't eat lunch still have this same slump. Additionally, the same slump does not usually occur after breakfast and dinner. Having a full belly *is* more likely to induce a relaxed state while being hungry is likely to increase alertness, but the midafternoon slump, unfortunately, is just part of our natural sleep cycle due to a surge of melatonin.

Whatever Works!

Ultimately, the scheduling of most ASMR sessions is going to be based on two key factors:

1. **Availability.** The session may have to occur after work, after school, or when your schedule allows.
2. **Need.** Although being relaxed is a great foundation for ASMR, many people may need an ASMR session to help them with a stressful day or moment. This means that some ASMR sessions may need to occur during less optimal times.

If you're offering ASMR services as part of a business, you may want to offer walk-in services, in addition to appointments, to allow for those moments when someone just needs an immediate de-stressing session.

Frequency

Another consideration to think about when you're scheduling is how frequent you want your ASMR sessions to be. Many people who enjoy ASMR like to experience it at least a few times a week or even several times a day. Having a bit of time elapse between sessions may have an advantage, though.

A small percentage of people who watch ASMR videos very frequently report that their ability to experience ASMR decreases or goes away, which is often referred to as "ASMR immunity." This does not imply anything negative about ASMR videos; this loss of ASMR can probably occur with any frequent stimulation of ASMR. The good news is that their ability to experience ASMR usually returns after taking a break of several days or a week. So you don't actually become immune but rather tolerant for a short time, so "ASMR tolerance" is a better term to describe the temporary loss of ASMR.

Although it may be frustrating, taking a break from ASMR inhibits excessive use. If you find your experience becoming less enjoyable than it was before, look at it as a built-in nudge that encourages you to take a break for a while. This decrease in enjoyment is probably due to a constant stimulation of receptors by specific brain chemicals like endorphins, oxytocin, or serotonin. These same chemicals are involved in all types of human relationships. When you see a loved one you have not seen in a while, you get an immediate surge of pleasure and happiness. That other person is triggering your brain cocktail of endorphins, oxytocin, and serotonin. The more frequently you see that person, the less you feel that immediate pleasure, and it may not return until there is another break between your visits together—hence the expression, "Absence makes the heart grow fonder."

Absence may also make the ASMR sessions more tingly. Scheduling ASMR sessions only once a week should prevent you from experiencing any loss of enjoyment. If you are having more than one session a week, you may want to keep track of the frequency of your ASMR sessions, as well as the strength of the ASMR in each session. This will allow you to see if ASMR tolerance is developing and the frequency of sessions that caused it. You may also want to track the frequency of all weekly ASMR; this includes videos, podcasts, unintentional triggers, and sessions. It is likely that all these ASMR sources can have an additive effect on ASMR tolerance.

INTENTION

Having appropriate intentions and some understanding can also help to make ASMR sessions successful. Thinking you can simply reenact your favorite ASMR video may be a little naïve. The creator of that video was probably alone and had several challenges that were edited out. You will have someone with you and all your fumbles will be viewed in real time.

Your initial ASMR sessions may be fraught with giggles, laughing, and not knowing what to do. This is to be expected, especially if you are with someone you feel close to, because your initial attempts at partner ASMR may feel silly at times. The point here is not to discourage you from laughing; having fun is a great side effect of attempting ASMR. The point is to prepare you to be aware that your first sessions may not be as smoothly executed as your favorite ASMR video.

If you both are laughing and smiling equally, then that may not be a problem. A problem could arise if one person is taking it more seriously than the other. Do your best to communicate to each other to prevent the session from becoming unenjoyable or frustrating. If you feel nervous or silly, let the other person know. If you wish the other person would try to focus more, then ask kindly. If either of you becomes upset, then the chances of ASMR occurring will be greatly reduced.

Once you get over the initial giggles or awkwardness, try to transition into a relaxed state of mind. It may even help to begin your first session, and perhaps every future session, with some type of relaxation ritual. Here are a couple of ideas:

- Sit across from each other or side by side and breathe in slowly through your noses, then breathe out slowly through your mouths. Try it for ten to twenty breaths, counting quietly between the inhale and the exhale. Closing your eyes may help you to focus and relax more quickly.

- Try progressive muscle relaxation, mindfulness meditation, yoga, or perhaps some relaxing music. (Remember that music may be inhibitive to ASMR, so it may be best to turn it off before starting the ASMR session.)

Once you both are relaxed and comfortable, try to shift into an ASMR-focused frame of mind that captures your role:

- If you are the one stimulating ASMR, then try to channel an ASMR artist you admire. Adopt his or her kind and caring disposition and continue the session with the focus that you think he or she would.
- If you are the one experiencing ASMR, then try to visualize yourself at a spa. Act the same way you would if you were being attended to by a professional. Remain serious and compliant but also maintain a friendly disposition and communicate about anything you like or don't like.

PREFERENCES

Preparing for ASMR should also include a discussion of preferences. Since both the giver and the receiver will probably be familiar with ASMR videos, it's a good idea to have a chat about favorite ASMR artists, channels, and trigger types prior to your first session. Make a point of creating two lists: one of favorite ASMR triggers and one of ASMR triggers to avoid.

Appendix A provides you with a handy menu of ASMR triggers to help guide your discussion.

Touching

There are a couple of triggers you can expect to see on most lists of favorites: whispering and light touches. Whispering can be a good beginning point because it doesn't need to involve touch. Although many people enjoy light ASMR touches, it's a more intimate trigger, so you want to do some work ahead of time to be sure the touching is within the recipient's personal boundaries. Prior to discussing specific touch triggers, begin by asking the other person how he or she feels about being touched. Most people are okay with being touched but not by just anyone. Touch is best received from people we trust, which may be from people we know well or from experts. Regardless of your relationship with the other person, ask if he or she would like to include or try touch triggers before beginning your first session.

If someone has mostly experienced ASMR through videos, then he or she may not have much experience with touch triggers. Be careful about doing a quick sampling of touch triggers. Hastily introducing someone to a bunch of touch triggers could create an awkward and nervous moment that could prevent ASMR. Instead, schedule a full ASMR session that begins with a relaxation technique in a comfortable setting and then slowly, gently, and carefully introduce the sample of different touch triggers.

Appendix B is an ASMR Personalization Form to help remind you of the questions you should ask about touch, as well as other important topics. The form is also a convenient way to keep track of their responses for future sessions.

Length of Time per Trigger

In addition to having a preference for trigger types, individuals may also have a preference for how long they want to be stimulated by each trigger. It is unlikely that someone will know exact times for each trigger prior to a session, but a 2017 study published in *PeerJ* shows that five-minute periods are a good starting point. So if you are planning a one-hour ASMR session, make sure you are prepared with a lot of ASMR triggers. Think of it like serving someone a big meal. Most people don't want to eat the same thing for an hour; they like a variety of tastes and textures, and they don't want to get too full in the first five minutes. Think of an ASMR session like a ten-course meal of small plates. Over time and as you develop a relationship with your ASMR partner, you might discover that some triggers are best as appetizers, some are best as the main course, and some are best as the dessert.

The meal analogy highlights another curiosity: how many triggers should be in each course? Additional research data about ASMR videos revealed that 47 percent of respondents prefer two triggers at once, 28 percent prefer three or more triggers at once, and 24 percent prefer one trigger at a time. This is also similar to a big meal. The main course usually has two or three items, and it is the central part of the meal. Single items, like a salad, appetizer, and dessert, are served individually at the beginning and end of a big meal.

So think about preparing your ASMR session like a big meal. Start off with a variety of single item triggers in a row, like bringing someone a beverage, a salad, and then an appetizer. These single ASMR triggers can be isolated moments of whispering, tapping, crinkling, unboxing, or light touching. The main course of the ASMR session can be a combination of triggers like an unboxing that includes tapping and whispering and perhaps a role-play with light touching and whispering. The winding down of the ASMR session can be several single triggers in a row, similar to ending a meal with a dessert, a coffee, and then a mint.

Appendix C has an ASMR Session Plan that you can use to create a multicourse trigger fest for each ASMR session.

TROUBLESHOOTING AND BUILDING A LONG-TERM PARTNERSHIP

The information you've just read in this chapter sets you up with the potential for great ASMR sessions. Go back and review this chapter anytime someone is having trouble feeling relaxed during a session or his or her ability to experience ASMR decreases somehow. There are multiple potential changes to consider:

- A new partner
- A different location
- A more focused intention
- A review of preferences
- A change in the frequency of ASMR stimulation
- A decrease in stress
- A clinician-patient discussion about other potential causes

Keeping your sessions fresh, interesting, and personalized is perhaps the best way to ensure long-term success with partner-based ASMR. Over time you will learn what works and what doesn't to create your ideal moments of deep relaxation.

Pause Point

Although this book is mainly focused on in-person partner ASMR, at some point you might be curious about making your own video, whether for you and your ASMR partner(s) to share or for sharing with the rest of the community on *YouTube*. You can use many of the tips, techniques, props, and scenarios discussed in this book to help you create an ASMR video. Combining this book with a camera, appropriate microphones, good lighting, video editing software, and some production magic is a great start to creating tingly videos.

PART 2
YOUR DIY ASMR TOOLBOX

Now that you understand more about the principles and practices of ASMR, you're almost ready to begin scheduling ASMR sessions. The next important topic to learn about is the wide array of trigger types you will be using to stimulate ASMR. This section of the book will cover the major types of triggers (vocals, sounds, touch, observation) and the specific tools you can use for each of these triggers. You will also learn specific and helpful techniques for each trigger type and for each tool.

Whether your sessions are formal or informal, paid or just for fun, this next section of the book will help prepare you for tailored and successful ASMR sessions with each individual. If you are new at partner ASMR, be careful not to jump right into it after reading the following chapters. Scheduling an ASMR session without practicing your techniques could result in a not-so-relaxing session. Practice each of the techniques as you read about them, perhaps initially alone and then with a friend. Practicing will develop your skills and increase your confidence—both of which are vital to successful ASMR sessions.

CHAPTER 3
VELVETY VOICES

FOUNDATIONS OF VELVETY VOICES

Perhaps the most important element of triggering ASMR via your voice is speaking in a relaxing way. You probably know how to do that already, but if not, just imagine you are trying to soothe a fussing baby. Or imagine someone you care for is heartbroken and needs comforting. What would your voice sound like? Yep, your voice would likely become softer, slower paced, more caring, and higher pitched.

Your relaxing voice communicates to another person that he or she is safe. When people feel safe, they feel trust toward you. When people feel trust toward you, they become relaxed. And when people have deep feelings of safety, trust, and relaxation, they are much more likely to experience ASMR.

Are all relaxing voices soft, slow, caring, and high pitched? Nope. There is wiggle room in a relaxing voice for variety, style, and personal preference. The next section will outline the ins and outs of speaking in a way that can trigger ASMR.

TRIGGER TIPS FOR VELVETY VOICES

Now it's time to learn some specific ways to hone and optimize your relaxing voice to trigger ASMR in someone else. And there is a lot to consider. How loudly will you speak? What tone will you use? What pace will you speak at? Will you use a higher-pitched voice or a lower-pitched voice? Do you have a relaxing accent? Should you try speaking in another language? When you think about it, the act of speaking has a lot of components. Considering them carefully will make you more likely to have a successful ASMR session.

SET AN INTENTION TO RELAX

Setting an intention to be relaxed might help you actually feel relaxed. To have a relaxed voice, it can help to begin with a relaxed mind. Your voice will project how you feel. The more you can relax yourself, the calmer and more confident your voice will sound.

> **"Take deep breaths before starting your session so that you yourself are relaxed. This helps you project a calmer voice."**
>
> —Somni Rosae, *YouTube* artist, Canada

Try this simple method for quickly inducing a relaxed mind:

- Sit in a comfortable position.
- Take one deep breath in through your nose, then release it through your mouth.
- Relax your shoulders.
- Allow your eyelids to get a little heavy, the way they would if you were really tired.

Do you feel relaxed? You can use this method, another relaxation technique, or listen to calming music to put yourself into a relaxing state of mind right before you begin speaking. Don't get *too* relaxed, though—you still need to remain alert enough to keep focused on the other person.

VOLUME

The most important trait of a relaxing voice is low volume. Aim for a voice that might be described as soft, gentle, light, or delicate. Keep in mind that the distance between you and the other person affects how he or she will perceive your volume. It can be easy to misjudge your volume if you're not consciously thinking about it. If you are right next to the recipient's ear, it is better to start too quietly and slowly increase your volume than to startle him or her by talking too loudly at first. Don't be afraid to ask the other person if you should speak a little more loudly or softly—this will help ensure you are using the best volume for that person.

TONE

The second most important trait of a relaxing voice is tone. Your voice should sound caring, supportive, or comforting—if appropriate to the topic or trigger. Caring tones are most important whenever you are providing personal attention. Don't force a caring tone, though; it should sound genuine to the other person. If you are simply reading, demonstrating, or explaining something, then a steadier tone may help relax the recipient. Be careful not to sound too monotone or dead-toned; your voice should still reflect that you care about the topic.

You may feel nervous as you begin doing your first partner ASMR sessions. That nervousness may be reflected in your tone, and the recipient might notice. Don't worry, though—this may not be so bad. Express your nervousness to the recipient. You are being real and genuine, and that can make the other person feel safe. On the other hand, radiating confidence with your tone and actions can also help the other person to feel safe. Confidence will come with practice and experience.

> "One of the most crucial techniques for vocally triggering ASMR in others (aside from speaking softly) is confidence. Whether the artist is folding towels, talking about gemstones, or performing an eye exam role-play, the most effective content creators tend to convey a sense of gentle authority when they speak. As I believe that a key element to fully enjoying ASMR is the ability to relax and be vulnerable, it follows that viewers would gravitate toward artists they feel they can trust."
>
> —Jellybean Green, *YouTube* artist, USA

PACE

Selecting the pace of your speech is an area in which you want to be flexible based on what the recipient wants. Generally, slower is better for many individuals. Be careful, though; talking too slowly may sound unnatural and disturbing.

> "Talking slowly, deliberately, and methodically seems to be a good delivery method. The topic is not as important as the delivery of it."
>
> —ASMR Muzz, *YouTube* artist, Canada

Feel free to speak at a normal pace if that fits your interest in or knowledge of the topic. A normal pace may naturally convey your enthusiasm for or expertise in a topic. Incorporate pauses to keep your words from sounding like a stream of consciousness. Faster speaking may stimulate ASMR in some individuals, but a faster pace can also be the result of feeling nervous or stressed. Be sure you feel relaxed so you don't talk too fast and project stress to the other person.

"It's okay to pause between words and sentences. It's okay to draw out some words, especially if it enhances a natural accent, regional or otherwise. Be genuine. If you're relaxed, I am."

—Katie, 48, female, USA

Whether you speak at a slow or normal pace, maintaining a consistent pace is important. Altering your pace may sound frenetic and alarming to the other person. A consistent pace will be best at relaxing someone's mind. If you are unsure of what pace to use, just talk at your normal pace. The other aspects of your voice will be good enough to make it relaxing. You can adjust as you speak if need be.

PITCH

Similar to pace, your pitch has flexibility. Generally, higher-pitched voices are perceived as less threatening and therefore more relaxing. A higher-pitched voice is often used by parents with their infants or when someone of lower rank talks with a person of higher rank. The pitch of the speaker is communicating that he or she is unlikely to be a threat.

On the flip side, a lower-pitched voice is associated with dominance and confidence. If you are talking about something that involves knowledge or skill, a lower-pitched voice may work well to relax the other person. The other person feels relaxed because your pitch conveys confidence, which elicits trust and therefore relaxation.

Imagine you are doing a clinical role-play to help the other person relax. You are the clinician; the other person is the patient. As the clinician, should you use a higher-pitched voice or a lower-pitched voice? The good news is that you can use either. A higher-pitched voice would communicate to the patient that you care about him or her and want to help him or her feel better. A lower-pitched voice would communicate that you are confident and have the skills to help him or her get better. Either pitch would help the other person feel relaxed and safe.

EYE CONTACT

What does eye contact have to do with voice? The combination of eye contact and a gentle voice can provide a very powerful feeling of personal attention. Eye contact may be incorporated into some situations involving voice. You probably won't be able to make constant eye contact if you are reading something or moving ear to ear, but you might make eye contact if you are rambling or sharing a personal story.

Keep in mind, though, that some people are not comfortable with eye contact. Sitting or standing behind the other person while you speak can be a simple solution for those not comfortable with eye contact. Just because someone may not be comfortable with maintaining eye contact does not mean they don't enjoy your gaze as part of the personal attention, however. Even if the other person is comfortable with eye contact, speaking from behind him or her makes it easier and less awkward for the other person to close his or her eyes and focus on your vocal triggers.

SPEAKING EAR TO EAR

Moving your voice from one of the recipient's ears to the other is a signature style of ASMR. The "stereo" nature and proximity aspect add more intimacy. Sitting or standing behind the other person while he or she remains seated in a chair may be the easiest and most comfortable position for both of you. To keep the other person fully focused on your voice, try not to touch him or her.

There are two basic ear-to-ear styles:

1. **Speak only when your mouth is next to the ear.** You can say a single word (e.g., a trigger word), a short statement (e.g., a line of a poem), or several sentences (e.g., rambling or reading) before moving to the other ear.
2. **Keep speaking while you are moving from ear to ear.** This second style works best when you are talking in continuous sentences or making sounds or speaking at a steady rate.

Encourage the other person to close his or her eyes. (This will also keep him or her focused on your voice.) Speak at a low volume, in a soft voice or a gentle whisper. As you speak, move at a consistent rhythm from ear to ear. Surprising the other person with an inconsistent rhythm may alarm him or her and break him or her out of the relaxed state.

OTHER CONSIDERATIONS BEFORE YOU START SPEAKING

Now that you have a handle on how you're going to speak, take a look at the setup of your session to be sure it's optimized for voice triggering.

SEATING

Prepare a place for the person to sit down. Make sure there is ample space for you to move all around him or her, especially space behind him or her for ear-to-ear vocalizations. It is important to make sure the seating is comfortable. A typical office chair works well. If you are using a wooden chair, then place a cushion or pillow on the seat and a thick, folded blanket over the entire chair. Make sure the person's feet are not on a cold or hard surface by placing a rug or pillow on the floor in front of him or her.

Pause Point

A floor rocker, sometimes called a gaming rocker or video rocker, is a chair that can provide a comfortable balance between sitting and lying down. This type of seating rests on the floor but allows the person to sit upright or lean back and stretch his or her legs out.

You may also be having a session with the other person lying down. This can be the most relaxing position for an ASMR session, although it's not appropriate for all sessions. A couch may seem like a good idea initially, but it will limit your access if you are touching the person lightly. In addition to a bed, other options include lay-flat futons, extra-large beanbag chairs, and of course piles of pillows on the floor.

WATER

Try to hydrate before a session to help prevent a dry mouth. If your mouth still gets dry during sessions, your first thought might be to grab some bottled water, but there are pros and cons to that choice. Every time you drink, the other person may hear the crinkling plastic of the water bottle. If he or she likes this sound, then that is a bonus trigger for him or her, but if he or she only wants to hear your voice, then switch to a glass of water or a solid drinking container.

Pause Point

You will also want to be aware of how you drink. Be careful not to sip, slurp, or gulp your water when you drink. Using a straw can reduce drinking sounds. Many people regard the sound of someone else drinking as disturbing. On the other hand, many people also enjoy it. Find out the preference of the person you are relaxing before starting the session.

The closer you are to the other person, the more likely he or she is to hear your mouth sounds. Another bonus of drinking water is that it may reduce mouth noises. If the person you are relaxing does not like mouth noises, then this could be important. (Of course, if the person does like mouth sounds, then proceed accordingly.) A note of caution, though: for some individuals drinking water can increase mouth sounds, so not drinking water could be more helpful. You may have to spend a little time investigating how drinking water affects your mouth sounds.

MANAGING YOUR VIEWING MATERIALS

If you are reading something or following an outline, then you will need to decide how you will view your material. Printing the text on paper has its pros and cons. If the other person enjoys the sounds of crinkling paper and turning pages, then you will be giving him or her a multisensory experience. If the person only wants to focus on your voice, then you can read the text directly from a laptop, tablet, or cell phone. A touch-screen device will offer the quietest option if you have to scroll through several pages.

Finding a place to put your papers, laptop, tablet, or phone so it is easily visible to read can be another challenge. One good trick is to buy a sheet music stand, which should easily hold these items. Music stands are relatively inexpensive, light, portable, and adjustable to various heights and angles.

SILENCE

Not using your voice at times also has value to ASMR sessions. If you think of being with your best friend or a loved one, you can visualize the comfort that can be expressed by silent moments. Express your comfort and relaxed state to the other person by including moments of silence, such as pausing and just allowing you both to be in the moment during a guided session or when telling a personal story.

CHECK YOUR BREATH

Finally, one additional tip that hopefully you don't need to worry about. You will be speaking or whispering in close proximity to the other person. You should therefore take some precautionary steps to ensure fresh breath. This may seem like silly advice, but it could be the one thing you are unaware of that could affect your sessions. For a touch of prevention, go ahead and freshen up with some toothpaste, mouthwash, mouth spray, or just a simple mint before each session.

WHISPERING: THE KEY VOICE TRIGGER

Whispering has been reported to be the most popular ASMR trigger, so you'll likely be using it with a recipient at one point or another. Curiously, it also seems to be a trigger many people can strongly dislike. In other words, don't add whispering to your session without doing your homework.

> **"When whispering to someone in person, it is key to maintain comfortability, communication, and safety. One of the techniques that I use is to direct my whispers away from the guest while being physically close to them. This prevents the guest from feeling my breath on their skin."**
>
> —Melinda Lauw, cocreator of Whisperlodge, USA

Ask your recipient ahead of time how he or she feels about whispering. If the recipient dislikes it, gently ask if he or she wants to try it again with you. Some individuals will learn they actually do like whispering but just from specific individuals, rather than disliking all whispering.

Pause Point

The first ASMR artist was inspired by watching video clips of people whispering from the TV show *Big Brother*. She created the first whisper-only channel on *YouTube* titled WhisperingLife (www.youtube.com/user/WhisperingLife).

Technique is very important to a relaxing whisper. To put it in exact terms, whispering is speaking without vibrating your vocal cords. Words are created solely by breathing out air and shaping it with your throat, tongue, mouth, and lips. Poor technique can easily result in the Broken Whisper, the Harsh Whisper, or the Evil Whisper—none of which are conducive to triggering ASMR.

The Broken Whisper

The Broken Whisper is usually done by someone new to whispering. The person accidentally allows his or her vocal cords to vibrate occasionally. This results in a whisper with occasional syllables that are significantly louder than others because the vocal cords vibrated. Relaxing your vocal cords and focusing on just using gentle air can help to prevent this. If it keeps happening, pause and put yourself back into a relaxed state of mind.

The Harsh Whisper

The Harsh Whisper is usually done by someone who is parodying a whisper. The person pushes air out forcibly during the whisper. This results in a whisper that is loud, audible, and not very relaxing. You can prevent this by pushing out the minimal amount of air, rather than the maximal, when you whisper.

The Evil Whisper

This type of whispering is usually done by an antagonist or evil character in a thriller or horror movie. The person whispers each sentence as one long breath while stretching out certain words. The words "Hello, Ross" would be whispered as "Hhhhellooooo, Rrrooossss" in one long breath. This results in a slower and breathier whisper, which can be spine-tingling in a bad way. A slowly spoken whisper can be relaxing, but the trick is to stretch out the time between the words, not to stretch out the words. Whisper at a slightly slow pace with occasional pauses after several words or each sentence.

The best way to create a relaxing whisper is to imagine you are whispering to express caring to another person or to share something meaningful about yourself. Imagine the recipient is your best friend or someone else you care deeply about. Visualize yourself whispering directly into his or her ear, over a phone, or while he or she is lying right next to you on a bed.

> **"A whispering voice only works on me if their enunciation is crystal clear. It has to be sharp; it has to sound like it would be your normal voice. It can't sound like you're running out of breath to whisper because it can make me lose focus."**
>
> —Somni Rosae, *YouTube* artist, Canada

TRIGGER TOOLBOX FOR VELVETY VOICES

Once you've set up the room and thought about how to speak, it's time to figure out what exactly to say. The following are some ways to plan the content of your voice triggers.

TRIGGER WORDS

Some individual words are widely reported to trigger ASMR. These trigger words are not isolated to any one language because it is the sound of the words that is the key, not their meaning. However, you may still want to avoid certain words or review them with the other person first. For example, *dentist* has a great sound as a trigger word, but it may take some individuals out of a relaxing state.

Pause Point

The best tools to create a list of trigger words may be websites that show you words that start with, end with, or contain the letters you specify. Examples include WordFind.com, Scrabble.Merriam.com, and ScrabbleWordFinder.org.

Here are some examples of English trigger words:

- Angelic
- Artist
- Ask
- Blend
- Bliss
- Bubble
- Castle
- Checkers
- Chocolate
- Coconut
- Cotton candy
- Crisps
- Didactic
- Glow
- Highlight
- Kiss
- Lipstick
- Lollipop
- Milk
- Package
- Popcorn
- Pssst
- Purple
- Relax
- Scratches
- Settle
- Silk
- Skeptical
- Sleepy
- Spectacle
- Stipple
- Sweatpants
- Tap
- Technical
- Tentacle
- Tickle
- Tingles
- Whisper
- Zest

These words can be read as a single list, as a repeated list, or as repeated words. It is common to pause two to three seconds between words, but the reading rate can vary based on preferences. Trigger words are ideal for ear-to-ear vocalizations because you can present them with a consistent rhythm.

Notice that the following consonants and combinations seem to be common and important in trigger words: *d, p, t, b, l, c, ch, ck, k, qu, x, s, sk,* and *st.* This means you don't need to spend a lot time trying to think up and test words to see if they sound tingly. You can just enter statements into an Internet search engine like "List of words that start with d" or "List of words that end with st."

Pause Point

The sound *sk* is its own trigger sound and was popularized by the ASMR artist Heather Feather (www.youtube.com/user/HeatherFeatherASMR). She was the first person to put it in an ASMR video on February 17, 2013.

Other places to find lists of words that start with specific letters are a dictionary and a phone book. The phone book also provides the option of reading names of individuals from the white pages or reading the names of businesses from the yellow pages. Dictionaries and phone books also provide a wonderful bonus: the crisp sound of thin pages being turned.

UNINTELLIGIBLE/INAUDIBLE SPEAKING OR WHISPERING

Since it is the sound of ASMR trigger words, rather than their meanings, that stimulate ASMR, just making up words with similar sounds also stimulates ASMR. It is called *unintelligible* or *inaudible speaking*. This is basically just rambling with made-up words. There are two advantages to using unintelligible speaking or whispering to trigger ASMR:

1. **You don't have to worry about the meaning of what you are saying.** You won't need to wonder what the other person thinks about the topic you are speaking about. In fact, this may be why unintelligible speaking can be so good at

relaxing someone. The other person can't think about and process what you are saying; his or her brain is only focused on the sound of your voice or your whisper.

2. **You don't have to prepare anything.** You don't need to hunt down information, choose a story, type anything up, or think ahead about your topic.

One important note: don't expect it to be easy to speak unintelligibly. On the contrary, it can be difficult to make up words without making repetitive sounds or accidentally saying silly words. Speaking in a low volume with a bit of a mumble can further hide any accidental real words. Over time, you will get better and feel more natural creating unintelligible words.

> **"Another most requested trigger on my channel is unintelligible whispering, and personally this is my favorite for tingles. Tips for others: don't rush it, speak slowly, and put some mouth sounds in there."**
>
> —Holly ASMR, *YouTube* artist, UK

Nonsensical speaking is a related concept. The slight difference is that you are using words that exist but making up a story that doesn't make sense. As with unintelligible speaking, the focus is on the sound of the words rather than the message. You can even pick out several trigger words to incorporate into a nonsensical story. This helps make sure the story is filled with ASMR-triggering words and sounds.

FOREIGN LANGUAGES

Foreign languages, spoken or whispered in a relaxing way, are wonderful ASMR triggers. Foreign languages and unintelligible speaking both allow the listener to focus solely on the relaxing nuances in your voice and mouth sounds, rather than being distracted by the meaning of the words.

If you are fluent in a foreign language, then you have a great tool in your ASMR trigger toolbox. The assumption here is that the other person is not fluent in the same foreign language. Your eloquent pronunciation and effortless flow can stimulate terrific ASMR. You can read something, ramble about something, or just make up a nonsensical story.

> **"I have always enjoyed languages that I don't understand, so I can just listen to the sounds of the speech and cannot be distracted by the meaning of the words. The more 'popping' sounds in words, like the *K*, *T*, and *P* for instance, are important triggers for me. So if a person pronounces these clearly, this is a plus for me."**
>
> —Jolien Morren, *YouTube* artist, Netherlands

Knowing a foreign language, even if you are not fluent, can also be helpful in stimulating ASMR. Instead of stimulating ASMR as an expert in that language, you can stimulate ASMR as a learner of that language. Listening to children learning to read is a strong trigger for many people. You can't fake being a child, but you can re-create a child learning to read by practicing reading in a foreign language.

There is triggering potential even if you don't have any training in foreign languages. Reading a foreign language that is totally unfamiliar to you is basically a script for unintelligible speaking. All you need to do is try your best to pronounce the words and keep your flow moving with confidence. Make sure that the person listening does not have fluency in the foreign language, or else your butchery of the language will pain his or her ears and stress his or her brain.

RAMBLING

Rambling is when you speak freely and openly in a personal way. You might talk about an experience you had a while ago, a belief you have today, a confession about something, or something about your day. Another simple word for it is sharing. Rambling is probably a strong ASMR trigger because it conveys a sense of comfort, trust, and safety between two individuals.

The key to rambling is being open and carefree. It is the way you talk openly with your family, friends, and romantic partners. The most intimate type of rambling is similar to chatting with a friend at a sleepover or even pillow talk with a romantic partner. You are speaking freely because you trust the other person and feel safe. Try not to overshare, though—sharing something too personal could make the moment uncomfortable.

Potential Topics

Rambling should be done without a script. The words should come from the heart, a vivid memory, an emotional moment, or the desire to express a feeling or belief. Topics to ramble about can be anything you have a strong but positive feeling about. Talking openly about a negative experience can also create a feeling of trust and stimulate ASMR. Be careful about crossing over from sharing to ranting or being too focused on a negative topic—that may stress the other person and inhibit ASMR.

The topics don't have to be personal, but the way you talk about the topic should be personal. For example, when you talk about your favorite movie to your best friend, it's probably in a rambling style, but if you were to talk about your favorite movie to your boss or a stranger, it would probably just be an explanation.

> **"I would prefer that the person stimulating my ASMR either talk or read about something that contains positivity and is uplifting in nature. Sure, they can acknowledge the bad, but then they must segue into the good that follows—leaving the receiver feeling positive and reassured that everything will be okay."**
>
> —Erin, 27, female, USA

Topics to ramble about include the following:

- **Personal stories:** a first date, a first pet, your first best friend, a personal achievement, a memorable moment in school, or a favorite moment with a sibling, friend, or romantic partner.
- **Confessions:** what you like and don't like about yourself, a crush, how you have changed over time, health goals, dream jobs, something you believe strongly about, places you want to travel, or items on your bucket list.
- **Favorites or opinions:** movies, bands, songs, celebrities, foods, TV shows, *YouTube* channels, podcasts, websites, clothes, electronics, cars, hobbies, or sports.

READING

Reading a story at bedtime is a time-tested method of helping a child fall asleep. Several core ASMR elements and triggers are a common part of this evening ritual:

- A soft voice
- A caring individual
- Personal attention
- Pages turning
- The light touch of leaning against someone you trust

You don't need to re-create the exact details of this bedtime scenario in an ASMR session, but channeling the care and love of a parent reading to his or her child can help enhance the experience for the recipient.

Selecting a topic to read about should not be a problem because a hallmark of ASMR is that it is more about how you speak than what you say. Of course, reading about a graphic murder case will be less relaxing than reading about a dolphin gliding through warm water. Be careful of stressful topics.

Pause Point

Would you prefer to have your daily news whispered to you? In 2016, *BuzzFeed* created a series of videos with Sarah Burton reporting the current headline news in a soft voice or whisper. The videos are available here: www.facebook.com/BuzzFeedNow/videos/265750713761421/.

Additionally, make sure to review any source material in its entirety before using it. The titles of stories, fables, plays, and poems can seem neutral enough, but the text might still contain adult themes or gruesome imagery that can bring someone out of a relaxing state. The backup plan to reading everything ahead of time is to be ready to skip over any unsettling parts of the material. If you can do it without pausing too long or gasping, then the other person may not even notice.

> **"I feel that any material used while talking or reading can trigger ASMR; however, I aim to use more positive material, which is far more beneficial for their well-being."**
>
> —CoconutsWhisper, *YouTube* artist, UK

Positive, comforting, and inspirational topics can be the most helpful at making the other person feel relaxed. Educational, informative, or interesting topics can also be helpful by distracting the person's mind from stressful thoughts. Even neutral or uninteresting topics can be helpful because the other person may be mostly entranced by your relaxing voice rather than your topics.

Consider the following options for reading material.

Fiction and Short Stories

Stories are the classic bedtime lullaby. They are great at engaging the brain, which helps distract the listener from the day's stress. Be careful not to read stories like a professional audiobook narrator. A professional narrator wants to bring excitement to the story and engage the listener as much as possible. You want to minimally engage the listener so he or she becomes relaxed. Keep your tone level and your volume low.

Fables and Tales

Fables and tales are great for all ages. They tend to have interesting story lines and moral or uplifting endings and are often the perfect length to be part of an ASMR session. Again, make sure you review the entire text of any fable or tale. The original versions of classic children's fables, as well as many other fables written long ago, often have dark tones with violence and death sprinkled throughout the story.

Plays

Plays are stories that are mostly driven by dialogue. This can create an immersive session for the listener as he or she may feel that the characters are present with him or her. Plays can be challenging in an ear-to-ear session, though. Ear-to-ear readings of a play can be confusing because you have to keep track of which of the many characters is usually spoken into which ear. The exception is a two-character play, which would be perfect for ear-to-ear readings.

Poems

Poems can also be a great addition to an ASMR session because of their variable lengths, and many have inspirational messages and imagery. Some poems have great rhythms and rhymes that can create a perfect and hypnotic ear-to-ear session. Practice poems prior to any sessions because they can contain strange words, rhythms, or rhymes that can surprise and interrupt the flow of a reading. The website Public-Domain-Poetry.com has more than 38,000 poems available in a large and easy-to-read font. If you sort the poems by title, the site also displays the number of lines in each poem, which can help when you want a poem of a certain length.

Song Lyrics

Song lyrics are very much like poems—they can be inspirational, and their lengths make them great for ear-to-ear sessions. Be aware that reciting lyrics from popular songs could cause more amusement than relaxation, and it could put a musical earworm into someone's head. Therefore, the best strategy may be to select lyrics from lesser-known songs and not to tell the other person they are song lyrics.

Lists

Lists of items can work well because you can speak them at a consistent rhythm. Their simple nature, like trigger words, also make them ideal for ear-to-ear sessions. Just enter any list idea you have into an Internet search engine, and you will probably find some great lists to read. Try to choose lists of things that bring comfort or ask the other person ahead of time for things that interest him or her. Topics for lists can include candy bars, fabrics, vacation spots, soups, dog breeds, flowers, and names of saints.

Recipes

Recipes can work well because food and ASMR are both about comfort. Make sure to select recipes based on the favorite foods of the other person. Another suggestion is to select recipes centered around foods that are great trigger words, like coconut. Reading the list of ingredients in an ear-to-ear style can also be ideal. Cookbooks and the Internet are obvious sources for an endless supply of recipes.

> **"I would like for the person stimulating my ASMR to read poetry or even song lyrics. Personally, I love science fiction and fantasy, so having someone read a book of those genres would be lovely. As for talking, I think I'd like for them to talk about calming topics or something that I can relate to such as a certain television show, travels, animals, or our pets."**
>
> —Karen Schweiger, CuddleInYourArms.com, USA

Instructions

A classic insult of something that is perceived as boring is "That is as exciting as the instructional manual." In the world of ASMR, instructional manuals can be bridges to the land of relaxation and sleep. Find some around your house or just search the Internet using the keywords *pdf*, *manual*, *guide*, *instructions*, or *specifications*.

Nonfiction

Nonfiction may not be as popular as fiction, but it is still very popular because people love to learn. Ask the other person what topics he or she enjoys learning about and seek out material on those topics. Nonfiction books, textbooks, newspapers, and many websites, including *Wikipedia*, offer lots of content.

GUIDED SESSIONS

Guided sessions include guided meditation, guided relaxation, and guided imagery. The process involves talking someone into a calm mental and physical state. Suggestions, gentle commands, and mental imagery are used to guide the other person to clear his or her mind, calm his or her thoughts, relax his or her muscles, slow his or her breathing, and visualize tranquil scenarios.

Guided sessions differ from most other ASMR triggers in an important way. Guided sessions rely on the meaning of the spoken words to guide the other person into a relaxed state. (Remember, other spoken ASMR triggers don't rely on the meaning of the words; instead, they rely on the sound and style of the speaker.) Combining the words of a guided session with the calming style of spoken ASMR can be a great way to coax someone into a deeply relaxed state.

Here are several ways to prepare for a guided ASMR session:

- **Use a prewritten script.** These can be found on the Internet by searching for the word *script* combined with *guided meditation*, *guided relaxation*, or *guided imagery*.
- **Write your own script.** Some individuals find this easy; others find it challenging. Be aware that simply telling

someone, "Clear you mind of the day's stress" can actually make some individuals focus on the day's stressful events. Have others read your scripts and provide feedback before using them in a session.

- **Improvise your guided session.** Over time, you will probably be comfortable enough to create a guided session as you speak.

Guided sessions could even be the first voice-trigger method to try if you are having an ASMR session with someone unfamiliar with ASMR. Someone may find trigger words, unintelligible speaking, or rambling too strange at first to be relaxing. Guided sessions done with whispering, gentle speech, or ear-to-ear vocalizations can combine something unfamiliar with something familiar for a more relaxing initial session.

USING YOUR VELVETY VOICE

Although your voice is only one of many ASMR triggers you can use, it may be your most valuable one. It is free, you always have it with you, it is unique to you, and it may be the best way to express a caring disposition. Another huge benefit of your voice is that it can and will be combined with other triggers you use. You can combine it with trigger sounds, light-touch triggers, and observation triggers, and you will also use it in role-plays. So make sure you invest the time into understanding and enhancing the utility of your valuable voice for stimulating ASMR.

CHAPTER 4
SOOTHING SOUNDS

FOUNDATIONS OF SOOTHING SOUNDS

Among the varied and strange ASMR trigger sounds are tapping, crinkling, squishing, scratching, and mouth sounds. Surprisingly, these sounds do have some common traits. They tend to be repetitive, methodical, gentle, made at a steady pace, and done at low and steady volume. In other words, these triggers have the opposite traits of sounds people usually perceive as threatening. Threatening sounds stimulate our alert response and inhibit relaxation, so they're not appropriate for ASMR.

The strongest trait of a threatening and nonrelaxing sound is a high volume, especially if the sound is sudden. Think of the crack of a whip or the slamming of a car door. A fast rhythm or pace, like the whirl of helicopter blades, also raises our alertness. Even a sound that starts slowly but then keeps increasing in pace will stimulate an alert response; this may be because it sounds like the object making the sound is coming closer. Very low frequencies, like the growl of a dog, can indicate aggression and danger. Curiously, very high frequencies, like the cry of baby or a scream, can indicate someone else is in danger, which also raises our alertness.

"When creating sounds like crinkling, tapping, and scratching, a good technique is (via practice) to make sure it doesn't get too loud or sharp, which will create the opposite effect of relaxation. Also, doing these trigger sounds for only a few seconds isn't long enough; each sound should have several minutes dedicated to it, and there should be a pattern or rhythm (for at least part of it)."

—ASMR Muzz, *YouTube* artist, Canada

To keep from stimulating the alert response, it is probably best to create trigger sounds with a low, steady volume and a slow, steady pace. The nonthreatening aspects of trigger sounds are probably important to their relaxing ability, but that doesn't fully explain the appeal of specific sounds. Perhaps we have been hardwired through evolution or conditioned during development to find certain sounds relaxing. For example, subtle crinkling sounds could replicate the sounds of family members nearby shifting their weight on leaves. Mouth sounds may signal that others have food. Sticky sounds may replicate the sound of sticky fingers from eating sweet fruits. Perhaps tapping sounds are similar to the heartbeat inside the womb or from the heartbeat of a parent holding you close.

ASMR trigger sounds may work by occupying your hearing to block out external noise. The term for this is *noise masking*, and it can be very helpful for relaxation and falling asleep. A steady and nonthreatening sound helps block out distant and unsteady noises that may alert and wake you. This is the reason many people use white noise, fans, and some nature sounds to help them sleep better. The advantage of trigger sounds over other masking sounds is that they can bring deeper relaxation and tingles.

TRIGGER TIPS FOR SOOTHING SOUNDS

Clearly, you want your ASMR trigger sounds to be soothing and relaxing. But how loud should you make them? Is it better to make them close to the recipient's ears or farther away? Should you use a slow pace or a quick one? Let's examine the many variables that affect your use of sound triggers.

VOLUME AND DISTANCE

A loud sound, just like a loud voice, is definitely not your goal. Begin each sound softly and then slowly increase the volume appropriately if you think it might be better a bit louder. Starting off with a loud and abrupt sound would not be a relaxing start.

Starting a sound right next to someone's ear can also be jarring even if the sound is not loud. Start creating the sound from a slight distance if possible, and then if you need to make the trigger louder, slowly bring the sound closer to the recipient without increasing the volume.

"Use slow movements and try to not create noises that are too loud. Fast tapping can be a trigger but it should be gentle and again, not too loud."

—Imperfect ASMR, *YouTube* artist, UK

RHYTHM

Rhythm is a term that can represent the tempo, speed, rate, pattern, or pace at which you create your ASMR sounds. It is safer to start at a slower rhythm and increase it. Be careful not to increase the rhythm in a steady, rising pattern. This type of sound can take someone out of a relaxing state because it sounds like something is quickly coming closer. Instead, increase the rhythm of a sound in phases. For example, tap at a slow and steady rate for the first phase and then tap at a faster but still steady rate for the next phase.

> **"The best way to trigger ASMR with crinkling and tapping is to consider dynamics and to treat the experience like a piece of music."**
>
> —Stephanie, adviser to Whisperlodge
> and creator of BitterSuite, UK

As you shift to a faster trigger sound, be aware that the volume of the sound will naturally increase as you create the sound at a faster rate. This is because you will be putting more force into making the sound as your hands and fingers move faster. Thus, if you start the sound close to someone's ear at a slow rhythm, then you will want to move a little farther away each time you increase the rhythm of the sound. Be careful not to make the rhythm too fast; fast rhythms can activate an alert response.

PITCH

The pitch or frequency of a sound may also determine how tingly it is for the recipient. Although both very low and very high frequencies can stimulate an alert response, sounds with a lower frequency may be better at stimulating ASMR. ASMR-sensitive participants in a 2017 study by Barratt, Spence, and Davis published in *PeerJ* reported that they preferred lower-pitched to higher-pitched sounds. Furthermore, more participants in the study reported achieving ASMR from tapping on wooden objects than tapping on ceramic objects. That might be because tapping on wood generates a lower-pitched sound than tapping on ceramic surfaces. If you don't trust your own ears, you can view the frequency of the sounds generated by your items using a spectrum analyzer.

Pause Point

Use the search term *spectrum analyzer* to download apps to your smart device to show you the frequencies generated by the sounds of your items. For general reference, low-frequency sounds are under 500 Hz, high-frequency sounds are over 2000 Hz, and between them are the mid-frequency sounds.

SEATING

You have some flexibility when it comes to seating arrangements. You can create sounds in front of the other person or from behind him or her. The advantage of being behind the other person is that it allows him or her to focus solely on the sounds, and it is a better location for you to do ear-to-ear sounds. You can also encourage the recipient to close his or her eyes to further become absorbed into the sound experience.

The advantage of being in front of the other person is that he or she can see your hand movements with the object, and you can make occasional eye contact. For some people, the combination of trigger sounds, hand movements, and eye contact may create a more tingly experience than sounds alone.

MAKING SOUNDS EAR TO EAR

Most items used to create trigger sounds are held in the hands while creating the noise, which makes them ideal for ear-to-ear sessions. The ideal position is to stand behind the other person while he or she is seated facing away from you. This will allow you to do ear-to-ear sounds by passing the item behind, over, and in front of his or her head. Human ears are very adept at locating sounds, and this will create an immersive multidimensional sound experience.

PRESENTATION OF ITEMS

Once you have assembled the items you will be using in the ASMR session, you'll need to decide how to present them to the recipient. It usually works best to keep them all out of view until you are ready to use them. This will keep the other person from getting distracted by looking at or thinking about the other items. You can hide them by keeping them in a box or laying them out on a table and covering them with a cloth or sheet. The plan is *not* to surprise the person with each item, though—that would not be ideal for relaxation. Instead, you can follow this three-step process to create the sounds.

Step 1: Introduce the Item Before You Use It

Speak in a gentle voice or whisper to keep the recipient relaxed. Hold the item in front of him or her and explain what it is, where you acquired it, a positive testimonial from another person you used it with, or anything positive about the item. Touch the item lightly in different areas to draw his or her attention to its details. The point is to establish familiarity and positive anticipation between the item and the person, which should increase the comfort level and enhance tingles.

Step 2: Create the Trigger Sound Entirely in View

This technique will further increase the recipient's familiarity and comfort with the item. You may speak during this second part if you wish or remain silent. Remember that silence can create comfort and it also allows the other person to focus on the sounds of the item.

Step 3: Create the Trigger Sound Out of Sight

You can have the listener close his or her eyes, you can move behind him or her, or both. The listener should be fully familiar with the item by now and therefore can comfortably focus on the sound it makes. You may begin this third step by saying something like, "While I am tapping, I want you to close your eyes and give the sound your full attention." Incorporating ear-to-ear movements while you remain silent should give the listener the most focused and immersive sound experience.

> **"Some good techniques in triggering ASMR are to just relax your body while doing it and try not to speak while performing actions. I find that waiting until you're done with the tapping for example, and then speaking, works best, at least for me. Speaking over the crinkling of the objects or scratching doesn't trigger me, and other people tell me it is an annoyance to them as well."**
>
> —Tony Bomboni, *YouTube* artist, USA

GUESSING THE ITEMS

The first step of introducing each item to the person is not a hard rule, especially if you both are already quite comfortable with each other and with using trigger sounds. You can insert a little fun into the session by adding a "guess the item" game to some future sessions. (First make sure the recipient wants to try this method.) Stand behind the recipient and encourage him or her to close his or her eyes. You can use items he or she has never seen or items he or she has seen or even tell him or her to match the sounds you make to a list of items.

Be aware, though, that you may be sacrificing a little bit of relaxation in exchange for amusement. The anticipation of the unknown objects and playing a game can put someone into an alert or excited state and slightly dampen his or her ASMR. As long as you have his or her approval, it will probably be an enjoyable experience. Guessing the items might not be an option you use frequently, but if your sessions with the same person are becoming too repetitive, it can be a fun diversion.

TRIGGER TOOLBOX FOR SOOTHING SOUNDS

Now it's time to talk about actual trigger sounds you can try. These lists are not exhaustive, but they will introduce you to some of the more popular items. Actually, almost any item in the world can be used to create trigger sounds. If you can tap on it, crinkle it, scratch it, handle it, move parts of it around, squeeze it, squish it, make it click, stick it to your fingers, chew on it, drink it, put it in a pile, or make any type of sound with it, then you can create trigger sounds with it.

Once you start creating trigger sounds, you will begin seeing that almost every item around you has potential to make good trigger sounds. You will also start noticing the nuances of materials that you never noticed before. It will seem like no two plastic bags crinkle in the same way, and every jar lid makes its own unique beautiful sound when turned back and forth. Your collection of items for trigger sounds will only be limited by your imagination and curiosity.

Building a large collection of trigger items doesn't have to be expensive. Your home is a great place to start looking for items. You can repurpose so many things as triggers. Search closets, the attic, the garage, toy boxes, and all those holiday decorations that may be hidden away. Even items you would normally throw away may be great for trigger sounds. The next place to browse for items is yard sales, thrift stores, and dollar stores. Once you have built up the foundation of your collection, you can then move on to purchasing specific items from local craft stores, department stores, or online merchants.

CRINKLING SOUNDS

Crinkling sounds are mostly made by crushing, flexing, or somehow manipulating a material in your hands. A common complaint about crinkling sounds is that they tend to be done too quickly and loudly. Keep this in mind and experiment with different speeds of crinkling with each person. Crinkling sounds can also be made by wearing something like latex gloves or a leather jacket and moving around.

> **"Only crinkling is a regular sound trigger for me. It can be different types of bags, plastics, or other material. Panning is key. Move from ear to ear. Make your movements slow and deliberate but not always predictable."**
>
> —WhisperHub, *YouTube* artist, UK

Examples of items for making crinkling sounds include the following:

- **Paper:** Crinkling sounds from paper can be created by handling it, folding it, turning pages, or slowly crushing it. There is a large variety of sizes, types, and thicknesses of paper, which results in different papers making different sounds. Sources of paper include books, magazines, catalogs, wrapping paper, tissue paper, and wax paper. There is even a free service that will deliver a variety of paper sources of various crinkle potentials to your residence every day. (This not-so-appreciated service is called junk mail, of course.)

- **Plastic:** Crinkling sounds from plastic are mostly made by handling it or slowly crushing it. You can make different sounds from plastics depending on the shape, thickness, and type of plastic. Sources for plastic include food wrap, sandwich bags, shopping bags, plastic bottles, and Bubble Wrap. A great source for an interesting array of plastics is all the packaging associated with anything you purchase, including the packaging material it may have been mailed in.

- **Leather:** Crinkling sounds from leather can be made by handling it or wearing it. Sources for leather sounds include baseball mitts, winter gloves, jackets, clothes, purses, and bags. Wearing a leather item while handling other types of items is a great way to combine different trigger sounds at the same time.

- **Latex:** Latex items can be worn or simply handled. Sources for latex include latex gloves, clothing, and Halloween masks. Be aware that some people don't like the smell of latex, and some are allergic to latex. Medical gloves made from different materials, such as polyvinyl chloride (PVC), nitrile rubber, or neoprene, could be used as an alternative or in addition to latex gloves. Additionally, clothing made from PVC can substitute for latex clothing.

- **Aluminum foil:** Aluminum foil can be handled or slowly crinkled. It is usually sold in standard thickness and heavy-duty thickness, which will produce different sounds. Many people either love or hate the sound of aluminum foil, so proceed cautiously.

Pause Point

Another interesting item you could wear or manipulate in your hands? A rain jacket. You could have the person hold an open umbrella while you tap on it and walk slowly around them in your rain jacket. This can create a wonderful rainy day theme of crinkles and tapping.

TAPPING SOUNDS

Tapping on items can be done with the soft pads of your fingers or with the hard tips of your fingernails. Each method provides a different sound, and both methods are popular for triggering ASMR.

What if your fingernails aren't long enough? Growing your nails may not be a good option due to time or preference. Luckily, there are several options for fake nails. The most realistic options are fake fingernails that are created to look and feel like real fingernails. These fake nails are often called press-on nails. One type can be glued, which is a good option for someone who wants to the keep the nails on for a week or more. Another type uses a non-glue, self-adhesive film, which makes the fake nails easier to remove than the glue-on nails.

There are additional options that don't look as realistic but will still work well for tapping. Nail rings, also called costume nails, fake fingers, fake claws, spike rings, talon rings, or claw rings, are among these options. Nail rings are usually metal and slide onto the tips of your fingers. They look like short talons and are usually worn as jewelry or as part of a costume.

Additional options require a little creativity and perhaps some trial and error. Look around your house or wander through some stores and look for anything that fits on the tips of your fingers.

Potential items that might work include thimbles, caps to large markers, and large paperclips.

Be aware of the frequencies associated with tapping on certain items:

- **Lower-frequency sounds**, which may be more relaxing to some, are produced by leather, wood, canvas, and cardboard.
- **Higher-frequency sounds** are produced by plastic, glass, ceramic, and metal.

If you are tapping with hard nails, try to tap lightly at first on items that produce higher frequencies. An upside of plastic, glass, ceramic, and metal items is that they are commonly cylindrical or dome-shaped (e.g., jars, bowls, and cups). These shapes can produce an amplified and resonating sound that can enhance an ear-to-ear experience. Just place the open side of the item near the ear and then very lightly tap on the other side.

Pause Point

Explore a large variety of objects and tapping speeds in "ASMR 20 Hours of Tapping Sounds for Sleep & Relaxation," a video by the ASMR artist MassageASMR (www.youtube.com/watch?v=wya8Qd5Z7y4).

Examples of items for making tapping sounds include the following:

- **Canvas:** You can use paintings or reprints on canvas for this trigger or purchase blank canvas stretched on a wooden frame. Tapping on canvas can be done with your fingertips or stiff paintbrushes. Channel your inner Bob Ross and tap out some white snow onto those happy pine trees.

- **Wood:** Sources of wood can include jewelry boxes, kitchen utensils, rulers, bowls, plaques, carved figurines, removable shelves, craft items, and handheld percussion instruments. A trip to a lumber yard will enable you to test and hear the differences among various types of wood. (The lumber yard may even have some scrap wood you could grab for free.)
- **Cardboard:** Your main source of cardboard is likely to be packages delivered from online merchants. You can tap on boxes of various sizes or cut out flat pieces of cardboard to tap on. Combining multiple layers of cardboard will change the sound of the tapping. Using binder clips to hold the cardboard layers together will make your layered cardboard easier to handle and store.
- **Plastic:** Sources of plastic for tapping include cups, bowls, kitchen utensils, food storage containers, measuring cups, bottles, toys, remote controls, small boxes, PVC pipes, and the housing of electronic items. Styrofoam is another type of plastic and can commonly be found in disposable coffee cups and packing materials.
- **Ceramic:** Ceramic materials include earthenware, stoneware, faience (such as Delft), bone china, and porcelain. Sources of ceramic include plates, cups, bowls, vases, and figurines.
- **Glass:** Sources of glass include drinking glasses, measuring cups, jars, baking containers, coffeepots, candle domes, light bulbs, and guitar slides.
- **Metal:** Sources of metal include pots, pans, cans, mixing bowls, measuring cups, kitchen utensils, camping dishes, water bottles, and housing of electronic devices.
- **Leather:** Sources of thick leather that are good for tapping include belts, baseball mitts, and wallets. Leather is not an item that is commonly chosen for tapping sounds, but its

nonresonating, low-frequency sound may be a preference for some individuals.

Pause Point

More items you can tap on: cell phones, hardcover books, holiday ornaments, and even the hard soles of dress shoes.

SCRATCHING SOUNDS

Some scratching sounds may work better if you have longer fingernails. If your fingernails are not long enough, see the options for fake fingernails mentioned in the section on tapping sounds in this chapter. You can also just drag your finger pads across items to produce a lighter brushing or stroking sound. Using a mix of scratching and finger-brushing motions on the same materials provides a richer array of sounds.

Examples of items for scratching sounds include the following:

- **Fabrics:** Sources of material include clothes, towels, sheets, upholstery samples, and rug samples. You could visit a craft or fabric store to test and create your ideal packet of fabric swatches.
- **Prior items mentioned:** Cardboard, wood, leather, and some plastics. Any item with a textured surface can also produce good scratching sounds.

Pause Point

Other curious items to consider for scratching sounds include beards or stubble and even cat scratching posts.

STICKING SOUNDS

Sticking sounds are made with anything that is made to be sticky, like tape. Sticking sounds can also be made with many items that are not naturally sticky, like when your fingers stick to the surface of an inflated balloon. The sticky noise produced by nonsticky surfaces comes from the moisture on your fingertips lightly adhering to a flat surface. The moisture comes from sweat glands, and the amount of sweat produced will increase when you are stressed. So being a little nervous or having naturally sweaty hands may help produce better sticking sounds.

Examples of items for making sticking sounds include the following:

- **Tape:** Types of tape include transparent tape, packing tape, double-sided tape, duct tape, and electrical tape. You can wrap pieces of tape, with the sticky sides outward, around the tips of your fingers, then touch them to each other or to other objects. You can also use a sticky-tape lint roller and roll it on your arm or other objects. To see a sticky-fingers video using various types of tape, watch the video by asmr zeitgeist on *YouTube* titled "STICKIEST ASMR ☆ Sticky Tapping & 3D Sticky Sounds ☆ Male Whispering" (www.youtube.com/watch?v=zbHBZodt9uo).

- **Substances:** Substances that can be placed on the fingertips to create sticking sounds include glue and the sticky substance that is on any of the types of tape previously mentioned. Wearing medical gloves before putting sticky substances on your fingers will make cleanup easier and add additional sounds. There is also a substance available in a tube called Mystic Smoke that can make sticky-fingers sounds along with a bit of smoke. To see a sticky-fingers video using smoke from a tube, watch the video by TirarADeguello on *YouTube* titled "Smoke and Mirrors ASMR" (www.youtube.com/watch?v=1HSFPjYtcPs).

- **Balloons:** Sources include latex balloons and Mylar balloons. Make sure the other person does not have an allergy to latex. There is another type of strange balloon for sticky sounds that is squeezed from a tube and inflated with a straw. To see a sticky-fingers video about the balloon from a tube, watch the video by Clareee ASMR on *YouTube* titled "ASMR Ultimate Sticky Fingers, Satisfying Sounds— Whispering" (www.youtube.com/watch?v=cvlxn4YMk1g).
- **Other items that your fingers may naturally stick to:** Leather items, gel masks, plastic wrap, and most flat plastic items like DVD and CD cases.

MOUTH SOUNDS

Mouth sounds fall into the love-or-hate category for ASMR triggers. Some people really enjoy them, but others will have a strong negative reaction, often referred to as *misophonia*. Mouth sounds can occur while speaking, eating, or drinking, or by just purposely creating them. Be sure to find out if the other person likes mouth sounds before adding them to an ASMR session.

Mouth sounds when speaking are mostly due to saliva and how much of it is in your mouth:

- **Less saliva:** When you become nervous, you produce less saliva that is also more viscous, resulting in a drier mouth that may create snappy sounds due to the stickiness of the saliva. Drinking some water will moisten your mouth but may not always reduce all mouth sounds.
- **More saliva:** A very wet mouth can produce squishy saliva sounds.

- **Saliva while eating:** Eating triggers increased saliva production, which mixes with the food. The liquid mixture easily produces wet, squishy sounds.

Examples of items and methods for making mouth sounds include the following:

- **Eating:** The initial sounds made by eating will depend on the food you select. Crackers will produce loud crunching noises, and soft cheeses will be very quiet. Be careful with foods that make loud initial sounds because these might be too abrupt for some individuals. (But some may prefer them.)
- **Chewing:** Eating sounds will change to chewing sounds once the food has been broken down and mixed with saliva. Chewing sounds can be immediately produced by gum or any semisoft foods.
- **Hard candy:** Eating hard candy allows you to combine the mouth sounds from saliva with the sound of the candy lightly hitting your teeth as it moves around. The candy is usually slowly dissolved rather than chewed or bitten. Dissolving a candy can be done as its own trigger sound or combined with speaking or whispering.
- **Pop Rocks:** Pop Rocks are a specific kind of candy that makes popping noises in the mouth as it dissolves in saliva. Using Pop Rocks as a trigger sound usually involves keeping the mouth open without chewing so the popping sounds resonate toward a microphone or a person's ear.
- **Lip smacks:** Lip smacks are created from saliva sounds when opening and closing the lips. The sounds can also be produced by pretending to chew something or pretending to dissolve a hard candy in your mouth.
- **Drinking:** The initial sound of drinking is due to the inflow of liquid through pursed lips, usually followed by a

swallowing sound. These sounds can be enhanced by sipping as you drink, gulping as you swallow, and then letting out an exhale after swallowing. Be careful, though; enhanced or exaggerated drinking sounds can also elicit very strong negative reactions in some people.

SQUISHING SOUNDS

Squishing sounds are usually created by squeezing a substance or object that contains liquid or has liquid-like properties. The most popular substance for creating squishing sounds is slime, which is its own phenomenon, due to the varieties of color, viscosity, texture, and sound that can be created.

Examples of items for making squishing sounds include the following:

- **Slime:** The slime is usually placed in a bowl or cup and then poked or held in your hands and squeezed. Slime can be purchased or created, typically by combining Elmer's Glue, borax laundry detergent, and water. Modifying the ingredients or adding other substances can create slimes with different sounds. Visit this website for helpful instructions on making a variety of different slimes: www.wikihow.com/Make-Slime.
- **Floam:** Floam is simply slime with small Styrofoam balls in it. As with slime, it is also placed in a container and poked or squeezed with your hands. You can purchase it or create your own by following a slime recipe and then adding the small Styrofoam balls.
- **Soapy sponges:** Squeezing soapy sponges over a bowl is a simple way to create squishing sounds. The sponges can be prepared by adding liquid soap to a wet sponge or by rubbing a bar of soap repeatedly on a wet sponge.

- **Lotions, oils, and creams:** Squishing sounds can also be created by applying a viscous substance to your hands and rubbing them together. These substances include hand lotion, body lotion, massage oil, hand cream, and Vaseline. The containers of these substances allow for additional trigger sounds like tapping and lid opening. As some lotions dry, their sounds may change from a squishing sound to a sticking sound, giving you two different sounds in one effort. Be aware that some of these substances will be easier to clean off your hands than others, so test ahead of time or wear medical gloves.
- **Fruit peeling:** Many large citrus fruits have thick peels that, when removed, create a sound somewhat in between a squishy sound and a sticky sound. Ideal fruits include navel oranges, grapefruits, tangerines, mandarins, pomelos, and ugli fruit. Be careful not to spray citrus spritz on the recipient as you peel the fruit.

ACTION SOUNDS

Action sounds are distinct sounds associated with common processes, such as turning pages, typing on a keyboard, or striking a match.

Examples of actions and items for creating sounds include the following:

- **Turning pages:** Page-turning sounds can be created from hardcover books, softcover books, magazines, and other sources. The size, material, and thickness of the pages can create very different sounds. Large hardcover books, like those found on coffee tables with beautiful photos inside, tend to have thick pages that produce a deep and rich page-turning sound. The pages of magazines and newspapers tend to have pages of medium thickness, and the thinnest pages, producing light and crisp sounds, may be found in some catalogs and phone books.

- **Cutting paper:** The sounds of cutting paper vary with the type of paper and size of the scissors. Deep and rich cutting sounds are produced with large scissors and cardboard or thick paper, which can include manila folders, construction paper, and high-quality wrapping paper. Lighter cutting sounds are created with smaller scissors and thin paper, which includes tissue paper, catalog pages, and phone book pages.

- **Folding paper:** Folding paper and creating creases with your fingertips or fingernails can also create enjoyable sounds. You don't need to create fancy origami shapes; you simply fold paper repeatedly for the sole purpose of creating folding sounds. Papers of different thicknesses will create different sounds.

- **Writing:** Various writing sounds can be created by using different types of pencils, ballpoint pens, fountain pens, crayons, markers, and chalk. Of these options, the most popular may be pencils and fountain pens, especially when coupled with the visual of writing in calligraphy or drawing a picture. Writing on different types of paper can produce different sounds, as can changing the surface under the paper. Writing on a single sheet of paper on a clipboard will create a scratchy sound. You can soften this sound by slipping additional sheets of paper or a piece of cardboard underneath it.

- **Hand and finger motions:** Hand rubbing, finger rubbing, and finger fluttering are also popular action sounds. You may need to place your hands close to the other person's ear so he or she can hear these subtle sounds.

- **Liquid movements:** Oil, water, or other liquids can be placed in an open container and poured back and forth into another container, or placed in a closed container and tilted slowly back and forth.
- **Opening lids:** Jars and containers with any type of screw lid can be used to create lid sounds. The lid is usually loosened and then repeatedly twisted back and forth. The lid may also be repeatedly removed and replaced onto the container. Different sounds are created by lids of different sizes and materials, which include plastic lids on plastic containers and metal lids on glass containers.
- **Striking matches:** Match sounds can be created with matchbooks, but wooden matches in boxes create a better array of sounds. The sound of wooden matches begins with the rattling of the matches in the box, followed by the firm striking of the match head on the side of the box, and concludes with the *whoosh* sound of the match lighting. Use appropriate safety precautions if incorporating matches into an ASMR session.
- **Typing:** Typing sounds are usually created on a keyboard meant to be used with a computer, but classic keyboard sounds can also be created with a typewriter. Typing sounds tend to be enjoyed more when done speedily. This may be because the fast sound conveys expertise and skill. Computer keyboards have two common styles that produce different sounds:
  - **Mechanical keyboards** tend to be connected to desktop computers and have raised keys that make a traditional *clack-clack* sound when used.
  - **Chiclet keyboards** tend to be built into laptop computers and have flatter keys that make a quieter *click-click* sound when used.

> **"I really like typing sounds on a keyboard.
> There is something about it that I
> find inherently very relaxing."**
>
> —Danny Docile, *YouTube* artist, UK

ITEM SOUNDS

Item sounds are the creation of a sound with one particular item or a group of the same items, like a pile of pencils or a bowl of beads. The sounds are created by placing the items in your hands, in a container, or in a pile and then moving them around.

> **"Pushing and moving buttons on gaming consoles
> usually brings out my ASMR. Also scratching
> weakly on a hard surface can be very relaxing.
> Be sure that the sound you're making is random.
> Swooshing of materials against each other can
> also be very relaxing if they do so randomly."**
>
> —Monika, 22, female, Norway

Additionally, most small items or objects that have moving parts can also create relaxing sounds.

Examples of items for these sounds include the following:

- **Pencils:** Pencil sounds are created by holding several at once or by rummaging through a pile of pencils. Traditional or colored pencils are usually used.
- **Beads and buttons:** Beads, buttons, or any small and hard items can produce soothing sounds. The items can be held in the hands, placed in a bag or sock, or placed in a bowl and rummaged through.

- **Dry rice and beans:** As with beads and buttons, sounds with dry rice and beans can be created by manipulating them in your hands, putting them in a bag or sock, or rummaging through them in a bowl.
- **Hair combs and brushes:** The item sounds for combs and brushes are created by playing with the teeth of the comb or the bristles of the brush. Additional trigger sounds can be made by tapping on any of the flat surfaces of these items.
- **Rubik's Cube:** Don't worry—you don't need to be able to solve the Rubik's Cube to create great trigger sounds. Just twist it randomly at different speeds and have fun.
- **Scissors:** The *snip-snip-snip* sounds of scissors are probably relaxing because they are reminiscent of a haircut. Move the scissors from ear to ear to evoke a haircut and switch between differently sized scissors to create different snipping and cutting sounds.

AN ORCHESTRA OF SOUNDS

The lists of trigger tools in this chapter can be misleading. It looks like each item creates one sound. Not at all. A single item may work well for several sounds. A small block of wood is great for tapping, scratching, and finger brushing. Take two small blocks of wood, and you can create additional sounds by tapping or rubbing them against each other. Place those two small blocks in a plastic bag and then tap on them, scratch them, or rub them together, and now you have an orchestra of sounds. Walk through your home or any store with an open imagination and some creative fingers, and you will discover endless options for wonderful trigger sounds.

CHAPTER 5
FEATHERY FINGERS

FOUNDATIONS OF FEATHERY FINGERS

Touch is a powerful trigger for the deeply relaxing sensations of ASMR. Haircuts, hair play, and gentle skin touching are commonly mentioned as early and favorite memories of experiencing ASMR. The observation, imagination, and anticipation of touch may even contribute to the tingly enjoyment of role-play videos featuring cranial nerve exams, makeup applications, and ear cleanings.

The magic of relaxing touch begins the day we are born. Holding and caressing a stressed newborn is a universal method of relaxation and comfort. Skin-to-skin contact between parents and newborns is even recommended by the World Health Organization for infant care. The appropriate cuddling and touching of infants has demonstrated decreased pain, decreased stress, improved mood, improved sleep, and improved parent-infant bonding. The release of endorphins and oxytocin has been shown to contribute to these benefits of touch.

Pause Point

The comforting nature of touch continues to be important as we grow older. Holding and caressing an injured, scared, or stressed child is an instinctual response for bringing comfort. As adults we may hug a distressed person, hold his or her hand, or just touch him or her lightly on the arm or back. The instinct to touch someone in distress and the reciprocal response of feeling comforted by touch never seems to go away.

Touch can indicate other positive things besides comfort too:

- **Social connectivity** is expressed by shaking hands, placing a hand on someone's shoulder, or touching another person on the back.
- **Joy** is expressed when we nudge each other while joking and hug each other to celebrate something or congratulate someone.
- **Affection** is expressed when romantic partners hold hands, cuddle, touch each other's arms lightly, or stroke each other's hair.

The benefits and joy of light touching are not just a human thing. Cats purr and dogs wag their tails in response to being gently stroked by people who care for them. One study even showed that when dogs and their caregivers are reunited after a separation, the stress hormones in the dogs only decreased if their caregivers touched them during the reunion. The light touching that occurs between monkeys and other animals (often referred to as grooming) has also been shown to be helpful for decreasing stress hormones.

> "One similarity that I see as a biologist is how blissful other animals look when they get groomed by their friends/packmates. I think ASMR may be a remnant in humans as I can imagine that inducing the feeling of ASMR in a friend could work in a bonding way."
>
> —Jolien Morren, *YouTube* artist, Netherlands

A 2015 ASMR research paper published in *PeerJ* reported that the strongest ASMR sensations were in the head, spine, and shoulders. The ASMR body map shown in the paper was similar to the touch body map in a 2015 study published in *Proceedings of the National Academy of Sciences of the United States of America* that showed the appropriate body area for touching by someone's mother.

Pause Point

Touch can increase stress hormones if done with inappropriate methods, to inappropriate areas of the body, or by inappropriate individuals. A 2015 research study published in *Proceedings of the National Academy of Sciences of the United States of America* reported that the participants trusted and enjoyed the touch of romantic partners, close friends, and close family members significantly more than the touch of strangers, acquaintances, and distant relatives. The study also demonstrated that the head, shoulders, neck, upper back, arms, and hands were the most appropriate areas for social touching.

Since touch is one of the strongest stimulators of comfort and relaxation, it makes sense that it is also one of the best ways to stimulate ASMR. You can expect light touching to be a highly requested trigger type. Touch may also be one of the strongest stimulators of discomfort and stress. We are selective about who touches us, when we are touched, and how we are touched. Careful and thoughtful technique will be the key to any successful ASMR session involving touch.

TRIGGER TIPS FOR FEATHERY FINGERS

You'll want to spend some time creating and refining your touch-trigger approach so it is pleasing to your recipients. Since you are initiating physical contact, it's important to be clear about what you'll do, respect boundaries, and be ready to change course midsession if need be.

CONSENT

People differ in how and where they like to be touched. Begin your first session by explaining how touch could be incorporated in this and future sessions. You want to provide a clear enough explanation so someone can visualize and understand what he or she may or may not be agreeing to. It would also be good to keep a written record of his or her response so you don't accidentally go against his or her preferences in a future session. You can use the ASMR Personalization Form in Appendix B to record someone's preferences regarding touch.

> **"To touch others safely, we need to ask for consent for every area we want to touch and explain how we are going to touch."**
>
> —Melinda Lauw, cocreator of Whisperlodge, USA

Touching

Some people will willingly and cheerfully agree to the inclusion of touch. Still, don't assume that this will be their preference at every session. This highlights a rule about touching you should employ with every person, at every session, and before every touch: ask for consent first. The recipient may have discovered at a prior session that he or she doesn't like being touched, he or she may not be in the mood to be touched at every session, or perhaps the person has a sunburn. Preferences can change for lots of reasons, so always ask for consent first.

Other individuals may seem cautious about being touched but express a willingness to try it. If so, you might want to explain in even more detail what the touch would entail so the person can make an informed decision. For example, you could combine the request for consent with an explanation so the other person has a full understanding of what you are going to do: "For our next activity, I'm going to graze my finger on the inside of your arm. Is that okay?"

> **"Basically, ask me what I want and listen to 'hear' what I say and incorporate that into our session. If I don't feel heard and safe, I won't be able to relax and receive. This is what I do for my clients and it works."**
>
> —Karen Schweiger, CuddleInYourArms.com, USA

It would even be a good idea to have a safety word or action. This may sound silly at first, but after a couple of uses, you both will agree it is helpful. Imagine that you are touching the other person in an uncomfortable place or in an uncomfortable way. You certainly don't want him or her to remain silent, but he or she may feel bad about saying, "I don't like that." So agree on a fun safety word or phrase as a gentle alert, such as *cheese grater*, *cactus*, *fire ants*, or *detour*. The person may prefer to use a safety action rather than a safety word. This does not need to be dramatic—something simple like raising a finger will work.

Not Touching

Some people may not want to be touched at all during an ASMR session. Don't take this personally; some individuals just have a significant discomfort with or aversion to being touched. You also shouldn't try to convince someone who prefers not to be touched to try it. Think of it like telling someone who doesn't like heights to try skydiving.

TOUCH ZONES

There are erogenous parts of the body that shouldn't be incorporated into ASMR sessions:

- The chest
- Pelvic regions (front and back)
- Upper leg regions (front and back)

There are also body zones that some individuals may want off limits due to extreme ticklishness or discomfort. Common areas include the armpits, sides of the torso, and soles of the feet.

Prior to your first touching activity, talk through a checklist of potential body areas with the other person:

- Hair
- Scalp
- Face
- Ears
- Neck
- Shoulders
- Upper arms
- Lower arms
- Backs of the hands
- Palms of the hands
- Upper back
- Lower back
- Lower legs
- Tops of the feet

Feel free to add personalized notes to the checklist for each recipient, such as favorite area(s) and special techniques for that area.

> **"I am highly particular of my hair, so no one other than my stylist touches my hair. In terms of the arms, it's gentle and light touches—almost featherlike—that have triggered the tingles. My upper back can handle touches with a little more pressure—tracing on the back is the best!"**
>
> —Somni Rosae, *YouTube* artist, Canada

CLOTHING

Encourage the other person to bring or wear touch-appropriate clothing. What exactly is touch-appropriate clothing? It will depend on the preferred body zones and methods for touching. Some individuals may be okay with being touched but are not interested in direct-skin contact. (It is also possible that *you* are not comfortable touching someone directly on his or her skin and request that the other person wear a long-sleeve shirt.) In those cases, form-fitting, long-sleeve shirts will allow for arm, shoulder, and back touching without direct contact.

On the flip side, you and the other person may be comfortable with direct-skin contact. The optimal clothing for this situation would be short-sleeve shirts or tank tops, which allow easy access to the neck, shoulders, and arms. If light touching of the lower legs is agreed on, then most pant legs can be easily pushed up or shorts could be worn.

Direct touching on the back can be a challenging situation. Touching someone's back by reaching under his or her shirt or having the other person remove his or her shirt should only occur between two consenting adults who are very comfortable with each other.

Choosing shirts of specific materials can make clothing less inhibitive of the touching experience:

- Thick shirts made of 100 percent cotton are probably the least conducive to transmitting the sensation of touch.
- Shirts made with a blend of cotton and polyester can be very thin and great at allowing heat and touch to be easily felt through the material.
- Shirts that are 100 percent polyester can also be thin and smooth enough to make it very easy for fingers to glide across the material.

HAND PREPARATION

Anything that may make the recipient reluctant to be touched can break the tingle spell. This includes being touched by dirty or untidy hands. It is likely that the other person will be looking closely at your hands when you are touching his or her arms or hands, so you want to be sure yours look presentable. The other person may also appreciate observing you use a hand sanitizer at the start of the session.

Cold hands and fingers are also not conducive to a relaxing touch-based ASMR experience. If you notice your hands are quite cold before a session, you could try immersing them in warm water or taking a shower to warm your entire body. If you still feel cursed by cold fingers in the middle of a session, then you can try incorporating a rice heat sock into your session. This can be created by putting uncooked (not instant) rice in a 100 percent cotton sock, knotting the sock, and then heating it for one minute in the microwave alongside a cup of water. The warm rice sock can be used to create crunchy ear-to-ear trigger sounds while at the same time warming up your hands. Learn more about how to properly create a rice sock at www.wikihow.com/Make-a-Rice-Sock.

LIGHT PRESSURE

Massage and touch-mediated ASMR have a lot in common. Both result in a deep and pleasurable relaxation due to a specific touch technique. However, most massage techniques involve firm pressure, whereas touch-mediated ASMR will involve light pressure. Think of how you might gently pet your cat or dog while it relaxes on your lap. You will use an even lighter touch than that during an ASMR session.

You will mostly use the tips of your fingers or your fingernails. Think of yourself as gently tracing something or touching a soft and fragile fabric. The pressure will be very light, and your movements will be at a slow or medium pace. Light touch in some areas can feel ticklish, so you may need to use a firmer pressure in some locations or with some individuals. You may use one finger, multiple fingers, or all your fingers, including your thumb. A light scratching with the fingernails may also work well in areas like the scalp and back.

> **"Be gentle when touching me to try and trigger my ASMR, but don't be *too* light because otherwise it will tickle me. Don't touch my legs, feet, under my arms, or my palms because I am ticklish. Be slow and use hands, makeup brushes, and oils."**
>
> —Imperfect ASMR, *YouTube* artist, UK

Use your fingers in creative ways. You can move your fingers in long, continuous strokes going from one end of a body area to the other. You can trace invisible patterns to create waves, swirls, and zigzags. You can also create pulses by grouping all your fingers and thumb together on the other person, then slowly and repeatedly separating them and bringing them back together, like a swimming jellyfish.

> **"Light touching of my face, hands, neck, and arms gives me tingles. Don't sexualize it, do give the person distance, and don't suffocate them with intensity."**
>
> —Holly ASMR, *YouTube* artist, UK

Be careful about touching in the same area for too long. Touching the same area can go from relaxing to numbing to annoying in a short amount of time. You will discover places on the other person that deeply relax him or her. Don't think of these as places to keep touching nonstop but as areas to visit often. Absence makes the touch grow fonder.

You don't have to be limited to just your fingertips. You can experiment with using:

- Your palm
- Your knuckles
- The flat surface of your entire finger
- The entire flat surface of your hand
- One hand or both hands at the same time

The key is to be creative and to enjoy yourself. Your enjoyment will add to the comfort and relaxation for the other person.

INCORPORATING TOUCH TRIGGERS AMONG OTHER TRIGGERS

Fitting touch into a session requires a little thought and advance planning. Because touch works best when the recipient is very relaxed and calm, it's probably not best to start a session with touch. Use other ASMR triggers at the start of the session to build the other person's comfort level and relaxation.

To ease into touch, you might want to combine it with other ASMR triggers. For example, a soft voice or whispering may be the ideal co-trigger when transitioning into a touch trigger. Combining trigger sounds with touching may be challenging because most trigger sounds also require the use of your hands. A little preparation and prerecording can overcome this challenge. You could record some trigger sounds and play them softly over speakers or headphones while touching the other person.

The transitional co-trigger may only be needed for initial touch activities. At some point you want to have the recipient focus on just a touch trigger without a co-trigger. You can have him or her close his or her eyes to give his or her full attention to the touch activity. You can remain silent during a specific touch activity, but if you are shifting to a different body area or to a different touch activity, then you should communicate softly with the recipient so you don't suddenly surprise him or her.

TRIGGER TOOLBOX FOR FEATHERY FINGERS

Once you've thought about consent, hand temperature, and transitions, you can start thinking about specific touch triggers you might want to try. As with other types of triggers, you will have lots of options, so plan on some trial and error.

HAIR

Early memories of ASMR for many individuals commonly include haircuts, hair brushing, and hair play. Even as adults (sometimes unconsciously), stressed or nervous people will sometimes soothe themselves by playing with their own hair. So you might find it a popular trigger that people ask for.

> **"Touching my head when getting a haircut, having my hair brushed, or getting a scalp massage stimulates my ASMR. My tips for triggering my ASMR through touch would be to use a gentle but consistent pressure and make sure your hands are warm. The ASMR I experience through being touched is stronger and more relaxing than ASMR I experience through videos on *YouTube*."**
>
> —Lindsay, 41, female, Canada

Keep in mind that many individuals get upset when someone messes with their hair or hairstyle, so make sure to ask for consent. If possible, let the other person know before arriving to the session that you may be messing up his or her hair a bit; that will keep him or her from wasting time on a nice hairstyle.

Be careful not to get your fingers caught in the person's hair. It may be best to brush your recipient's hair, or ask him or her to brush it, prior to using your fingers in it. Because hair has a wide variety of textures and lengths, not all of the following activities will be suitable for all hair types. Use the ones that seem most appropriate and pleasurable for your recipient.

Examples of touch activities for the hair include the following:

- **Hair touching:** Touching someone's hair is a popular trigger for relaxation. You can tousle it, stroke it, run your fingers through it, or lightly touch it with a variety of pressure and speed. As long as you are careful, there is almost no wrong way to do this.
- **Hair accessorizing:** Add and remove hair accessories. Useful items include hair clips, barrettes, hair combs, hairpins, scrunchies, elastics, ponytail holders, headbands, hair wraps, and bun shapers. Additional possibilities include hair rollers, hair curlers, and curling rods.
- **Hair shaping:** Add substances to shape and play with the recipient's hair. Substances can include water in a spray bottle, mousse, gel, gel wax, gel spray, wax, sculpting lotion, hair spray, hair moisturizer, molding cream, and hair balm.
- **Hair braiding, updos, and buns:** Hair can be separated into strands for braiding and also twisted or pulled up into an updo or bun. Examples include three-strand braid, four-strand braid, fishtail braid, French braid, cornbraid, cornrow, pigtail, French braid updo, quick twist updo, and topknot updo.

You may be worried because you are not a professional hairdresser. That is not a problem. The primary enjoyment for the other person is due to you touching his or her hair. Just make sure the other person understands that his or her hair may not be appropriate for a formal gathering when you are done.

SCALP

Running your fingers through someone's hair usually results in your fingers running across his or her scalp. Having your scalp rubbed or touched can be so soothing that it is another common self-soothing activity. Head or scalp touching can be helpful for any hair type—long hair, short hair, or no hair.

Pause Point

Cafuné is a Portuguese word that means "to caress someone's head or run your fingers through his or her hair as a way to relax him or her or help him or her fall asleep."

Examples of touch activities for the scalp include the following:

- **Scalp touching:** Push your fingers to the base of the hair so your fingers are directly touching the scalp. You can make creative patterns or move your fingers randomly, but be careful of creating hair tangles. Feel free to alter your pressure and try very light scratching.
- **"Climbing Everest":** Start with your fingers at the base of the scalp and then slowly keep applying light pressure while you move your fingers toward the top of the head. Once at the top, pull your fingers off the scalp and bring them back to the base of the scalp at the same location or a different one. Climb the mountain again; repel back down; repeat.
- **"Tingly Rain":** Mimic raindrops with pitter-patter motions of your fingertips. You can do this with your fingers directly on the scalp or just tapping through the recipient's hair. Change the speed and firmness to mimic different types of rain. You can start with a light rain, increase it to a heavy downpour, and finish with occasional large drips falling off tree branches. You can also run your fingers down the recipient's neck, shoulders, and back to mimic water runoff.
- **"Egg on the Head":** A game sometimes played with children. It usually involves placing your hands in a ball on

top of someone's head, opening your fingers to simulate a cracked egg, and slowly moving your fingers down the sides of the head like a runny yolk. To keep it relaxing rather than entertaining, it may be best not to tell them you are simulating a broken egg on their head.

FACE

Encourage the other person to close his or her eyes before you touch his or her face so he or she can relax and not try to focus on anything. You can extend the facial touch to include the ears and neck. Be careful around the lips; they can be sensitive or ticklish.

Examples of touch activities for the face include the following:

- **Face touching:** Face touching can include the temples and ears. You can trace aspects of his or her face, make creative patterns, or move your fingers randomly.
- **Face tapping:** Use your fingertips to lightly tap on different areas of the person's face.
- **Eyebrow touching:** You can also give special attention to the eyebrows via some light stroking or soft rubbing.
- **Face lotion application:** You can apply small dabs of face lotion or moisturizer and spread it using different finger patterns.

SHOULDERS, BACK, ARMS, AND LOWER LEGS

The shoulders, back, arms, and lower legs have a variety of sensitive areas. Be most careful around the armpits and the backs of the knees because touching there can certainly jolt some people out of a relaxing state. The underside of the arm tends to be more sensitive than the top of the arm. For many individuals, the top of the arm and the legs will have some hair that will provide a different sensation than just touching bare skin. To access the recipient's back, you can have him or her sit backward in a chair or lie on his or her stomach if you have an appropriate location.

"When someone gently touches my hands, arms, shoulders, or back in random patterns, I experience very strong ASMR. When someone caresses my back, arms, neck, or hands, every muscle in my body goes limp. Fingers are best, they apply just enough pressure to really be felt."

—Monika, 22, female, Norway

Examples of touch activities for shoulders, back, arms, and lower legs include the following:

- **Shoulder, back, arm, and leg touching:** You can run your fingers in long, straight lines; make creative patterns; or move your fingers randomly. You can also give special attention to any hair via some light touching or gentle tugging.
- **Trace the vessels:** Some individuals have visible blood vessels in these areas, especially the arms. You can gently trace these with your fingers. These surface vessels may be less prominent if the person is cold or nervous. Warming up the room or warming up the arm directly with a warm cloth can help bring more blood to these vessels.
- **Connect the dots:** Some individuals also have freckles, moles, and other small marks. Connect them by grazing your finger from one to another. You can also count them in a soft voice or whisper.

- **Shapes and forms:** Drawing shapes, letters, numbers, or words makes it easy for you to come up with patterns and may just seem like random patterns to the other person. You could invite the person to guess the shapes and forms aloud or quietly to himself or herself, but that could be too engaging and detract from the relaxing moment.
- **Body lotion application:** You can apply small dabs of body lotion or moisturizer and spread it using different finger patterns.

HANDS

Fingers and palms are the most sensitive areas of the hands and some of the most sensitive areas of the body. Hands can also be the most common way germs are spread because they touch so many things, so making sure both of you have clean hands is important. Feel free to encourage the recipient to wash his or her hands or use hand sanitizer before beginning.

People can also be very conscious of their hands, especially if you are about to focus on them. If someone is concerned about sweaty hands, then you can begin by having him or her use an alcohol-based sanitizer, which will dry out the hands temporarily. If your recipient is concerned about having dry hands, then you can offer him or her hand lotion or moisturizer.

Examples of touch activities for hands include the following:

- **Hand touching:** Hands are another sensitive area that some people really enjoy having touched. You can trace the edges of your recipient's fingers, make creative patterns, or move your fingers randomly.
- **Tracing palm lines:** Simply trace the various creases in the person's palm.

- **Shapes and forms:** Similar to what was previously mentioned, you can draw shapes, letters, numbers, or words on the back and front of the hands. Turning it into a guessing game may make it more fun, but less relaxing.
- **Hand lotion:** You can apply small dabs of hand lotion or moisturizer and spread it using different finger patterns.

A TOUCHING ENDING

You and your partner may find some of these initial sessions with light touching awkward. Additional sessions will reduce this, and so will another strategy—role-plays. In Chapter 9, you are going to learn about role-plays that include light touching. Instead of just tracing the creases in someone's palms, you can do it as a palm reader. Instead of just touching the marks on someone's arm, you can do it as a dermatologist. Role-plays provide structure and purpose to the touching, which could help you both feel more comfortable. Over time, you will discover what works best for you and for each of the individuals in your sessions.

CHAPTER 6
TINGLY TOOLS

FOUNDATIONS OF TINGLY TOOLS

Chapter 5 highlighted the soothing and relaxing effects of touch that exist from the day we are born and continue throughout adulthood. The chapter also explained that the comfort of a gentle touch is best done by people we trust, with appropriate technique, and to appropriate places on our bodies. Touching another person with your fingers can be a powerful way to stimulate ASMR.

All that information is also important to this chapter—with one new perspective. You can touch someone *without* using your fingers. Touching someone directly with your hands is very personal, and some recipients (or you) might not be comfortable with it. Using an object, device, or tool is still very personal, and all the important perspectives from Chapter 5 still apply. Instead of your fingers or hands, though, you can use hairbrushes, makeup brushes, gentle fabrics, and of course, the popular head tingler device. Here are some reasons that indirect touch might be a good option:

- **It can ease the transition to direct touch.** Touching someone directly can be awkward and a little uncomfortable at first for both individuals. The other person may be fine with direct touching, but it still may be best to progress from indirect touch to direct touch. For early ASMR sessions, create an initial comfort and connection through indirect touch, and that may result in the first direct touch being a better experience.

- **You can create different sensations.** Fingers definitely provide their own magical sensations, but they don't offer a lot of tactile variety. Gentle brushes, soft feathers, delicate fabrics, and the metal prongs of the head tingler device provide a wide range of interesting and relaxing sensations.

TRIGGER TIPS FOR TINGLY TOOLS

As you begin experimenting with using tools, it's a good idea to have some background knowledge of what objects work well and why. Then you can develop your sessions in a more thoughtful and intentional way.

CONSENT AND CLOTHING

The best starting place for learning about important trigger tips for tingly tools is to review all the trigger tips for feathery fingers in Chapter 5. Almost all these prior trigger tips apply to tingly tools also. These tips include the following:

- Asking consent before touching
- Knowing the appropriate areas for touching
- Encouraging the other person to wear clothing suitable for touching
- Washing your hands
- Being aware of touch pressures and patterns
- Combining touch with other trigger types

If the other person prefers not to be touched directly, you do not need to ask why. Regardless of his or her reason, your immediate and supportive acceptance of his or her position is what means the most.

In addition to all these trigger tips, consider the following when it comes to tools.

CLEAN TOOLS

An upside of using objects is that they usually have fewer germs on them than our hands. However, they still do have some germs on their surfaces. This means that brushes, fabrics, metal-prong head tinglers, and any other objects have the potential to transfer germs from one person to another. The germs can include bacteria, viruses, lice, and other transmittable microbes. This is such an important concern that places like hospitals, day-care facilities, and spas have sanitation standards and procedures to minimize the spread of germs.

There are several methods you can use to prevent the transfer of germs, explained next. Overall, you may end up using a combination of these methods. Some items, like sponges and brushes made with real hair, can't be sanitized, so your methods will depend on the object along with the preferences of the other person. Being rigorous about only using clean objects will make the other person feel comfortable, which is a terrific foundation for a relaxing and tingly ASMR session.

Have the Other Person Bring His or Her Own Objects

This may sound inconvenient, but there is an additional upside besides hygiene. The person is already comfortable with these objects and may experience ASMR more easily with them. You could even save him or her the hassle of bringing the objects every time by storing them if you have the space. If he or she is unsure of what objects to bring from home, provide a list of items. The person may find some of the items already in his or her home or purchase them.

Purchase Each of the Objects for Each Client

You can buy some items in bulk and then have the other person reimburse you. You might be surprised at the low cost of some items. You can purchase the metal-prong head tinglers for less than $5 each, and you can buy large, beautiful feathers for less than $1 each. You don't need to purchase new objects for every session, just for the first session with each person. As previously stated, the other person can take the objects home or store them with you if you have the space.

Use Disposable Items

Items like cotton balls, bathroom tissues, and cotton-tipped swabs each create a unique and delicate sensation. The other person may feel comforted while watching you take a new item out of its bag or box, use it, and then dispose of it. On the other hand, some individuals may find that wasteful. You can give the person the option of reusing his or her own items in future ASMR sessions or not using disposable items at all.

Sanitize the Objects Between Uses

Check with the manufacturer of the item to see if it has an approved sanitation procedure. As an alternative, you may be able to clean the objects with soap and water, with disinfecting or antiseptic wipes, or with hospital-grade disinfectants certified by the Environmental Protection Agency. You can sanitize the objects right in front of the other person or have them labeled or stored in a way that demonstrates they have been sanitized. It won't convey confidence if you reach into a shabby and unorganized box of objects and say with a hand wave, "Oh, don't worry; this item is clean."

Pause Point

The Kansas Board of Cosmetology put out a newsletter that provides a concise yet comprehensive explanation about cleaning and disinfecting procedures for instruments used in hair salons. A lot of the information may help you to keep your tingly tools properly sanitized. You can access it here: www.kansas.gov/kboc/Newsletters/Cosmetology%20-%201st%20Quarter%202016.pdf.

ALLERGY AWARENESS

A big safety risk you could have with partner ASMR is triggering an allergic reaction in the other person. People can be allergic to various tool materials like metals, animal proteins, latex, and other substances. This means you should know two things: if the other person has any allergies and what substances are contained in any materials you use.

The presence of a metal in most objects is usually obvious, but make sure you know the types of metals in each item. If you incorporate medical gloves into an ASMR session, try to use ones made from nitrile because they are latex-free. Paintbrushes and other brushes could be made from animal hairs. Although animal hair does not trigger allergies by itself, the hairs could still have animal proteins stuck to them.

Overall, animal proteins could be your biggest concern because animal proteins are almost everywhere, and many people are allergic to them. This is an important reason to always wash your tingly tools between individuals so you don't transfer animal proteins from one person who owns pets to another person who is allergic to animal proteins. If any animals have been in the space you will be using for the ASMR session, then alert the other person. Some of the items you use may actually be pet toys or grooming tools; make sure never to use those items with any pets prior to using them in an ASMR session.

The prior chapter mentioned the use of lotions. Be aware that there could be substances in those lotions that may trigger allergies. Additionally, the scent of lotions, as well as perfumes, colognes, and aromatic oils, can elicit a strong negative reaction in some individuals with a fragrance sensitivity. Be sure to discuss any potential allergies and sensitivities with the other person. You can use the ASMR Personalization Form in Appendix B to record someone's allergies and sensitivities.

PRESENTATION OF THE TOOLS

The presentation process of an item for touch-mediated ASMR is similar to the process and reasons for the presentation of items for sound-mediated ASMR. (See Chapter 4.) You can keep the items out of view before using them to prevent the other person from being distracted by a pile of items. You won't be surprising him or her but instead following a presentation plan similar to the one you utilized for items used for sound-mediated ASMR.

Step 1: Introduce the Item

First, introduce the item before you touch the recipient with it. Speak in a gentle voice or whisper to keep him or her relaxed. Hold the item in front of him or her and explain what it is and where you acquired it, provide a positive testimonial from another person you used it with, and explain how it has been appropriately cleaned. The point is to establish familiarity and positive anticipation between the item and the person, which should increase his or her comfort and enhance his or her tingles.

"For all materials and objects I use, I enjoy introducing them to my guest in a very slow and matter-of-fact way. I will introduce a makeup brush, for instance, by showing it to my guest and tracing with my fingers. I outline different parts of the brush as I explain them. For example, 'This brush has a wooden handle, a silver barrel, and a dome-shaped head.'"

—Melinda Lauw, cocreator of Whisperlodge, USA

Step 2: Touch in Plain View

The second step will be to touch the other person on his or her hands or arms so he or she can view you using the item. This will further increase familiarity and comfort with the item.

Step 3: Touch Out of Sight

The third step will be to touch the recipient in a place he or she can't view or have the recipient close his or her eyes. You may begin this third step by saying something like, "While I am tapping, I want you to close your eyes and focus fully on the gentle sensation on your skin." You can help your partner focus on the touch sensation by remaining silent, or you can provide a multitrigger experience by continuing to whisper or speak gently.

TESTING NEW TOOLS

The understanding and practice of ASMR is still so new that there aren't any devices specifically designed for stimulating it. The downside of this is that you can't search for ASMR-stimulating devices at any online merchants or in any local stores. Instead, you can use the lists in this chapter, be creative, and discover your own ASMR-stimulating devices.

Before using any tool on another person, make sure to test it first. You might trigger apprehension rather than relaxation if you say to someone, "I found this strange item at a yard sale yesterday. Let's see how it feels." When you acquire a new item, have someone else try it on you first. Get a second opinion on the item by then trying it on another person but not as part of an ASMR session. You want to be able to introduce every new item into an ASMR session with, "A friend and I tested this out, and we thought it was wonderful. Let me know if you enjoy it also."

When you are testing a new item, you are screening it not just for how relaxing it is, but also for any potential safety issues. These safety issues include inspecting the items for sharp edges or splinters as well as using the item in a safe way. Do not use anything with prongs or points around the eyes. Also be aware that the angle at which you use the item can affect how it feels. Items with prongs, points, or sharp edges shouldn't be pushed forward on the skin like a snow shovel but dragged backward with a gentle pressure.

GAMES AND PATTERNS

You don't always need to present the items to the other person first. Once you think the other person has a consistent comfort with being touched with different items, you can change up your sessions to make them interactive. Feel free to play the "guess the item" game initially mentioned with using items for sound-mediated ASMR. Make sure to get the approval of the other person first. You can have the person close his or her eyes, or you can touch the items to his or her back. You can use items the recipient has never seen or items he or she has seen and let him or her try to match the feel of the object with ones he or she is familiar with.

You can also play some of the same games mentioned in Chapter 5 for feathery fingers:

- The other person can close his or her eyes while you draw something lightly with an object.
- Draw shapes, letters, numbers, or words, and the other person then can try to guess what you drew.
- Create playful patterns by tracing blood vessels or connecting marks on the skin like freckles and moles.

TRIGGER TOOLBOX FOR TINGLY TOOLS

As with other triggers, you'll have a wealth of options for tingly tools. Each one offers a different tactile sensation, so you can create a session full of varied but relaxing sensations.

SCALP MASSAGERS

Scalp massagers are known by several other names, including head tinglers, octopus massagers, head massagers, head spiders, and head scratchers. The device has a handle attached to twelve long metal prongs with small plastic knobs on the ends. The metal prongs are shaped like a small birdcage without a bottom. The device is placed on top of someone's head and slowly pushed down and pulled back up so the ends of the prongs massage the scalp.

There are several variations of scalp massagers:

- Battery-powered versions create vibrations in the metal prongs.
- Some have similar names but different shapes.

- Some scalp massagers have plastic prongs in the pattern and are the size of a hand to provide a stiffer sensation.
- Additional scalp massagers have short silicone bristles for a softer sensation and are also called scalp massage brushes.

Pause Point

The first head tingler was called "the Orgasmatron" and was created by Dwayne Lacey, who registered the design in 1998.

Although most of these devices are named or promoted for massaging the scalp, they can also be used on other parts of the body.

> **"I think the 'spider' head massager is always a winner! I've managed to trigger ASMR-type sensation in many of my family and friends using this head massager."**
>
> —WhisperHub, *YouTube* artist, UK

HAIRBRUSHES, COMBS, AND PICKS

Hairbrushes and other hair grooming devices may require you to touch the other person with your free hand in order to steady yourself, arrange hair, or address some other situation. This is an important difference from almost all the other tools in this chapter. If your goal is to not touch the person directly, then make sure to test each item with someone to see if it can be used without direct touch. You don't want to be with someone who is not comfortable with direct touch and then accidentally place your hand on his or her head while you brush his or her hair.

Another difference with these hair grooming devices is that they mostly work on the hair and perhaps partially on the scalp. Don't think that these items are only appropriate for individuals with long hair, however. The goal here is not to actually groom the other person but to provide his or her hair and head with a tactile sensation. Use a wide variety of brushes, combs, and picks with everyone, especially if they have short hair or no hair.

> **"Hair brushing and stroking someone's face with makeup brushes are my most requested triggers. I think this is because I feel comfortable and like doing this for people. So I feel that the person gets more out of it."**
>
> —Stephanie, adviser to Whisperlodge
> and creator of BitterSuite, UK

You actually want to be the most selective and careful with longer hair. Select the tools least likely to cause you to pull or tug on the hair with too much force. It may be difficult for you to judge the right tool for different hair types and lengths, so feel free to ask the other person to help select the best grooming items. You can also have the recipient brush his or her own hair before beginning to remove any tangles.

Hair grooming tools can work well on other parts of the body. The large variety of these items can result in a buffet of sensations. These items are widely available and relatively low priced. Hairbrushes have the largest assortment of styles favorable for tingly tools. Types of brushes vary by shape and bristles and include round brushes, paddle brushes, detangler brushes, cushion brushes, vented brushes, boar-bristle brushes, and soft-bristle brushes.

MAKEUP BRUSHES

Makeup brushes are usually extra soft and available in a huge variety of styles. Eye, lash, and brow brushes can be relatively small while foundation brushes are usually the largest. The bristles of makeup brushes may be all the same length, tapered to a point, or spread out flat in a fan formation. Don't limit the use of these brushes to the faces of females; use them with everyone and on other body areas.

PAINTBRUSHES

Paintbrushes can provide a much larger array of sensations than makeup brushes. Paintbrushes can be tiny like some very small makeup brushes, but they can also be many times larger than the largest foundation brush. Some paintbrushes have bristles almost as soft as makeup brushes, and some have a much stiffer and coarser feel, which you would never want in a makeup brush.

A drummer's brush is an item that can provide a stiffer sensation than a paintbrush. It's made with long nylon or wire bristles, and it is used on drums and cymbals in some jazz compositions. This type of brush can provide a welcome and different sensation from the other types of brushes.

FUZZY AND SMOOTH FABRICS

Natural and synthetic materials that feel the most soothing on our skin tend to be extremely soft or fuzzy. The softest of these materials include fur, cashmere wool, angora wool, and thick fleece. You or the other person may have concerns about using real fur due to cost, animal welfare, and animal allergies. The obvious alternative to real fur is fake fur, also called faux fur, synthetic fur, craft fur, or vegan fur. There are also wool alternatives, known as faux wool or vegan wool.

Fuzzy Options

Fuzzy materials like faux fur may be the best of the soft materials to use in an ASMR session. All you need is a small piece of material to gently caress the other person's skin. Luckily, faux fur comes in many shapes and forms useful for ASMR sessions, such as strips of craft fur, pom-poms, hats, scarves, earmuffs, collar wraps, shawl shrugs, leg warmers, boas, and wrist wraps. The most useful and readily available form is probably gloves or mittens with faux fur on the palm side. If you have gloves or mittens with the faux fur on the back only, then you can wear them backward on the opposite hands to put the faux fur on the palm side.

Another suitable material is chenille, which is soft and fuzzy. In fact, the word *chenille* is the French word for "caterpillar" because this material looks and feels like the soft hairs on a fuzzy caterpillar. Chenille is created from natural cotton fibers or from synthetic fibers like rayon or acrylic. You can utilize chenille as an ASMR trigger in the form of yarn, pom-poms, powder puffs, scarves, gloves, and dusters with handles. Some of the most convenient forms of chenille for ASMR sessions may be carwash mitts and carwash brushes. These items usually have dozens of soft, dangling strands of chenille.

Smooth Options

Natural and synthetic materials that are extremely smooth are also soothing to the skin. The smoothest of these materials include silk, satin, and sateen. These materials have a similar feel but different compositions and weaves. Silk is a natural protein fiber produced by silkworms. Satin is a synthetic fabric usually made from polyester, nylon, and rayon and may include some silk. Sateen is a little less smooth than satin; it is made from cotton and may include some satin.

Compared to soft and plush materials, silky-smooth fabrics don't have as many forms suitable for an ASMR session. A little creativity can help, though. Cut the arm or leg off a piece of clothing made from one of these smooth fabrics. You can use this fabric in three different ways to create different sensations:

- Drape it on someone's skin and slowly drag it for a gentle caress.
- Put your hand inside it and touch the other person's face, arms, and back through it.
- Have the person insert his or her arm inside it and gently touch him or her through the silky-smooth fabric.

SCRATCHING TOOLS

Tools that can create a slight scratching sensation may also be a welcome addition to some ASMR sessions. Back scratchers are an obvious choice for their ease of use, and they are available in wood, plastic, or metal. They also have a variety of functional ends and styles. Some can add a bit of fun to your session because they may be shaped like bird talons, bear claws, deer antlers, zombie hands, or lawn rakes. The important thing, though, is that each different shape probably provides a slightly different sensation.

Another helpful tool for providing slight scratching sensations are fake nails. These are not the ones that stick over your own nails to look like real fingernails. Instead, these are the nail rings that were mentioned in Chapter 4 to help you make tapping or scratching sounds. These nail rings simply push or clip on to the end of your fingers and are also known as costume nails, fake fingers, fake claws, spike rings, talon rings, or claw rings.

FEATHERS

A feather duster—a bundle of feathers with a handle—seems like it was designed to be a tingly tool. You can also use individual feathers; they are easy to hold, heavenly soft, and available in a variety of sizes and textures. You can purchase the real feathers of ostriches, geese, turkeys, ducks, roosters, guinea fowl, pheasants, and chickens online. You can also purchase fake feathers, more often listed as imitation feathers. A feather boa can be another fun form to stimulate tingles with feathers.

Pause Point

Tool tip: create actual feathery fingers by attaching a small feather to each finger using tape, bandages, or small elastics. You can also create feathery fingers by inserting the quill portion of the feathers into fingerless gloves or medical gloves with holes in the fingertips or tuck the quill into rings on each finger.

CAT TOYS

Some cat toys may also be ideal for ASMR sessions, especially the ones known as "teasers." These toys have a long handle, stick, or wand attached to a soft item. The soft item may be a group of feathers, a soft fabric, or a long fuzzy boa. If the soft item is connected to the handle by a long string, then you may find it more useful to remove the soft item and just hold it in your hand.

TINGLY TOOLS ARE EVERYWHERE

You've probably realized from this chapter that tingly tools are everywhere—cotton balls from your bathroom and that soft, dangling tassel that was attached to your graduation cap will work too! Just be creative, be aware of safety issues, and start filling your toolbox with tingly tools.

CHAPTER 7
TRANQUIL TREASURES

FOUNDATIONS OF TRANQUIL TREASURES

Watching someone handle and explain a treasured object can be a strong ASMR trigger. The item may be part of a collection, from a local shopping spree, or an online purchase, or it may just be a favorite possession. Each item is typically picked up, displayed carefully to the other person, and explained in a quiet but joyous tone. The explanation usually conveys the person's strong interest in, excited discovery of, deep affection for, or expert knowledge of the item.

"I would sometimes binge-watch luxury wallet and purse unboxing videos. The fact that someone is paying such close attention to a delicate object gives me intense tingles. Removing the packaging to expose the luxury brand item, such as a Louis Vuitton wallet, triggers me a lot, especially because I really like that kind of wallet. So the fact that I like the item being showed, I think somehow triggers my ASMR even more."

—Tony Bomboni, *YouTube* artist, USA

This show-and-tell style of presentation is popular in ASMR videos. Videos of this style usually have the word *unboxing, haul, collection, favorites,* or *show-and-tell* in the title. Although the presenter may be excited and delighted to share the items with the viewer, the vocals are still soft or whispered. Another common trait of the videos is taking a little extra time to gently crinkle the shipping package or product packaging, as well as to tap on the item or on the box that contained it.

HOW PRESENTATIONS FIT INTO ASMR

Like most ASMR triggers, show-and-tell presentations involve personal attention because the treasured items are usually displayed and explained to the viewer. The difference between these presentations and other types of personal attention is that the attention is mostly focused on the items. The treasured items are clearly in the spotlight, and the viewer is just passively observing and listening instead of being actively engaged or receiving most of the attention.

There are additional aspects of show-and-tell presentations that are common to other ASMR triggers:

- The presentation is a focused and personal moment that is occurring between two individuals in a safe and quiet environment.
- The sharing of a treasured item or collection signifies trust and is an expression of intimacy.
- The disposition and vocals of the person are enthusiastic or even-natured without any threatening aspects.
- The touching and presenting of the items is done with great care and usually includes tapping or crinkling sounds.

If some core aspects of ASMR triggers are safety, comfort, and trust, then it makes sense that the open sharing and presentation of treasured items can initiate tingles.

CONNECTIONS TO OTHER SPECIES

When most other species collect and protect piles of items, it is because those items have value to their survival. Those treasured items are vital resources that are usually only shared with other members of the species they have close relationships with. Sometimes the sharing of the resources is done to create new relationships.

> **"Find what's interesting about the object
> to you, and lean into that interest."**
>
> —Andrew Hoepfner, cocreator of Whisperlodge, USA

So someone's collection of glitter stickers is strangely comparable to a squirrel's pile of buried nuts at the start of winter. Both are precious items that are only shared with key individuals to create or strengthen a bond between the individuals. It may seem silly to compare stickers to food necessary for survival. But if someone has invested a lot of time gathering and protecting something, then we inadvertently give value to it and become interested in it.

> **"I am triggered by the sounds, or the explanation,
> of what they're doing. The objects do not matter.
> Let's say someone is showing their makeup
> collection. I would prefer that they describe
> each object, open it, and show the object. The
> whispering and the noises of the jars/tubes/
> etc. opening would be triggering for me. Explain
> what you are doing in deliberate whispers, tap on
> objects, and clearly show me what the object is."**
>
> —Juliet, 32, female, USA

The greatest value of show-and-tell is the presenter's interest in their treasured items. Viewers who are already interested in the items will be further mesmerized. Viewers who did not have a prior interest in the items could be drawn in by the presenter's deep focus on the item. A viewer may or may not initially care about the items in an unboxing video or a haul video, but the presenter's focus and desire to display it carefully and share information about it creates an alluring interest in the viewer.

TRIGGER TIPS FOR TRANQUIL TREASURES

It may seem daunting to think about finding a cool treasure to present, but you probably already own many suitable items. Consider the following advice to help you narrow down your options.

SOURCES OF TREASURE

Your first step is to acquire a treasure. You will want one that will be suitable for ASMR sessions, so an antique car isn't going to work well. Choose some special items that you can hold in your hands and show to the other person. The significance of the items may be their rarity, nostalgia, beauty, usefulness, curiosity, or enjoyment. The items should be so meaningful that you are excited and quite willing to talk about why each one is so special to you. Peek at the list in the "Trigger Toolbox" section at the end of this chapter, and you will most likely see some items that you already own that should work well.

Don't worry if you look through the list and nothing jumps out to you as some treasured item. Review the list again with the following three categories of treasures in mind:

- A **traditional collection** is a group of similar and treasured items, like a baseball card collection.

- A **themed collection** is any group of items that fit into a topic you create, like your favorite items in your kitchen, items that make your life easier, items you received as holiday gifts, items in your purse or car, or your favorite snacks.
- **Individual favorite items** might include your favorite winter hat or favorite book.

If you still feel like you may not own anything that you consider special enough to excite you, then go hunt for a treasure. A shopping spree of any kind is likely to result in treasured items. Go to local stores, yard sales, thrift stores, *Craigslist, eBay*, and online stores. Look for quirky items, useful items, and items that you might amass into a traditional collection. Be extra alert for interesting items that also can allow you to create soothing trigger sounds.

TALKING ABOUT THE ITEMS

As long as you are presenting items that genuinely interest you, then you will have a lot to say. Your tone and pace may be enthusiastic and fast because you are excited to share your items with the other person. Your tone and pace could also be more even and slower because you are carefully explaining interesting or meaningful aspects of the items. Just let your interest in or knowledge about the items guide your disposition and vocal style. The most important aspect of your vocals is to keep your volume low by speaking quietly or whispering.

As you speak, keep your focus on the items. Display each item clearly to the other person as you talk about it but without addressing him or her. The viewer should be totally passive while you speak at him or her rather than with him or her. The interest and focus are not on the items or on you but rather on your interest in the items. It is even okay not to make eye contact frequently because you are so interested in looking at and explaining the details of the object. Allow the other person to become passively absorbed in your passion for the items.

> **"A great technique for triggering ASMR by physically manipulating items (whether it's by crinkling, tapping, scratching, sorting, or unpackaging) is to treat the item of focus as though it's precious and adored. I could enjoy watching someone lace up an old shoe if it's done with the same deference as handling a Fabergé egg. The experience of watching the gentle, deliberate handling of an object gives me what I call 'empathy tingles.'"**

—Jellybean Green, *YouTube* artist, USA

This also means that games may not be a good idea for this type of ASMR. In some prior chapters, you were encouraged to play guessing games to add some fun to the session. A guessing game with your collection would actively engage the other person and break the magic spell of passive and deep relaxation. This doesn't mean you should never do it. Try it at some point and then ask the other person afterward what he or she thought. Your partner might share that he or she had fewer tingles but found it more enjoyable, or perhaps the direct personal attention heightened the tingles. Experiment and find out.

SHOWING THE ITEMS

You have several options for how to display your treasured items. One popular starting point is to begin with your items in some type of package or box. This is common to many unboxing and haul videos and can add a little mystery prior to the unveiling. More importantly, it adds the opportunity for crinkling and tapping sounds.

> **"When unboxing, have a pair of scissors so that cutting the tape is not too loud and so that the box can be opened easily—seeing and hearing someone struggling to get past the parcel tape is not relaxing. The slower and more deliberate the movements, the better it seems to be for the people watching it."**

—Imperfect ASMR, *YouTube* artist, UK

On the other hand, the one type of treasure you may want to start in open view is the traditional collection. The significance, effort, and value of a large collection of Bolivian thimbles is lost if the other person doesn't see them all at once at the start.

How close you are to the other person is another important consideration when displaying your items. This is not a public demonstration; it is a personal moment of sharing. Sit directly in front of or directly next to the other person and keep all your items in reach. A 2017 research study published in *PeerJ* reported that the preferred distance for watching an ASMR activity is twelve inches (thirty centimeters). If you were holding a figurine in your hands, this would be about the distance from your hands to your face. So sit close enough so the other person can view the item as if he or she were holding it.

If your collection items are out in the open, it may not matter if they are in a large random pile or a precise arrangement. Even rummaging through a pile of items can be relaxing for the other person. Interestingly, there is some research that shows how you put down the items can affect ASMR. Placing items in a predictable sequence or order was reported in the 2017 *PeerJ* study to be more likely to increase tingles than placing the items down in a random fashion. So whether you are picking up an item from a pile or from organized display boxes, carefully return each item in an organized and predictable pattern that the other person can observe.

"It is a good idea to plan ahead and decide in which order you will be presenting the items. I like to have stronger-sounding material at the beginning then continue on with quieter sounds as it is possible that the viewer may be falling asleep. Unboxing items can be unpredictable, so I tend to open the box beforehand and then repack it for the video. It's also helpful to open lids for example before the video as they can be very loud during filming."

—CoconutsWhisper, *YouTube* artist, UK

HANDLING THE ITEMS

Handling the items may be as important as talking about the items. It is okay to continue to handle and display an item while not saying anything. Your silence while you continue to touch, inspect, and gaze at the item further demonstrates your deep interest in it. The reverse situation may not work as well. Continuing to talk about an item while not handling, displaying, or gesturing to it could be less tingly. In other words, it is okay to "show" without "tell," but try not to "tell" without "show." The focus needs to be kept on the treasured item.

"Trace slowly or handle the items featured with more care than in an everyday situation."

—Amanda, WhisperSparkles ASMR, *YouTube* artist, UK

You may also want to use precise manipulations when you handle the items. The way you handle an item reflects your interest in and the perceived value of it. This means that you should pick up and handle each item with great care. For example, slowly removing a makeup brush from its plastic sleeve prior to presentation can enhance the experience. Being too purposeful, though, can make your movements robotic, so handle the item with a balance of genuine interest and natural movements.

How long you display the item is also important. The worst thing you can do is to be too rushed. Show every detail and side of the item while also sharing whatever comes to mind. The challenge is that you may have collected two thousand erasers and feel compelled to explain them all in one session. Don't. The rushing will be frenetic, disorganized, and not relaxing. Choose some items ahead of time or set a time limit. There will always be future sessions to talk about more erasers.

"I watched an unboxing video on *YouTube*. What seemed to trigger my ASMR was the lack of talking, the crispness of the sounds, the methodical slowness, the tapping and rubbing of the box and packaging material, and the examining of the item from several angles."

—Kristina, 44, female, USA

Showing someone your collection can be a multisensory experience because he or she will hear your voice, see you handle the items, and hear you handle and touch the items. Think of it like an ice cream sundae. The item is the ice cream, your voice is the whipped cream, and then to really make it amazing, you sprinkle additional trigger sounds on top like hot fudge, nuts, and a cherry.

Some items and how they are handled will have their own sounds, like the crinkling paper of comic books, the jostling of jewelry, the sounds of plastic protective covers, and the opening of nail polish containers. Some items may not make sounds by themselves, but that is the magic you can add. In some cases, it is as simple as the additional sounds of your sweaty and sticky fingers on the item, a delightful sound to many. In many cases, it is tapping with fingertips or fingernails on different parts of the item.

TRIGGER TOOLBOX FOR TRANQUIL TREASURES

You need to make two decisions before incorporating a tranquil treasure into an ASMR session: what you will present and how you will present it. Review all the following suggestions and then make your decision based on your available items, supplies, the preferences of the recipient, and your time limits.

PRESENTATION STYLE

Here are some ways to consider showing your item(s):

- **Visible item:** Presentation begins with an item openly visible to the other person. Ideal if time is limited and you only want to present a single favorite item.

- **Mystery package:** Presentation begins with an item or group of items in a plastic shipping package. Plastic package is crinkled prior to removal of each item. Ideal for individuals who enjoy plastic crinkling sounds.
- **Mystery box:** Presentation begins with an item or group of items in an unmarked box. Box is tapped prior to removal of each item. Ideal for individuals who enjoy tapping sounds.
- **Unboxing:** Presentation begins with an item in a marked box. Prior to opening the box, the imagery and text on the outside of the box are discussed while tapping on the box. Every item in the box, including accessories, cords, and warranty cards, is removed one at a time, then handled and discussed. Ideal for presenting any item that is sold in a marked box.
- **Haul:** Presentation begins with several items in a paper shopping bag. Each item is carefully removed from the bag one at a time and presented. Ideal for presenting multiple items that were recently and perhaps locally purchased because they'll often come in a paper shopping bag like that. Also ideal for those who enjoy paper crinkling.
- **Collection:** Presentation begins with many items openly visible to the other person. Items may be in a disorganized pile or in a precise and structured arrangement. Rummaging through the items is encouraged for extra tingles. Ideal for presenting a traditional or themed collection.

> "I really enjoy watching people sort through jewelry because I love to see all the different pieces that people have and it is a monotonous process that calms me."
>
> —Hannah Carter, 30, female, USA

ITEMS TO PRESENT

Here are some ideas for what you could present:

- **Common collections:** baseball cards, Pokémon cards, coins, stickers, magnets, stamps, pins, souvenirs
- **Media and accessories:** music (vinyl albums, cassettes, CDs), movies (Blu-ray, DVD, VHS), video games (discs, cartridges), headphones, earphones, mobile devices, phone cases
- **Print items:** comic books, magazines, hardcover books, paperback books, postcards, holiday cards
- **Cosmetics:** nail polishes, lipsticks, eye shadows, eyeliners, blushes, lip glosses, lip balms, applicators

> **"My ASMR could be triggered by watching someone sort small wooden objects, going through a makeup collection, or cleaning any type of small collection."**
>
> —Brandi, 37, female, USA

- **Grooming items:** brushes, shampoos, conditioners, lotions, perfumes, colognes
- **Clothing and accessories:** shoes, hats, bandanas, T-shirts, socks, scarves, jewelry, hair accessories, belts, bags
- **Home items:** board games, card games, craft supplies, toys, stuffed animals, candles, pens, sewing supplies (colorful spools of thread, buttons, shiny sequins)
- **Food:** candies, candy bars, teas, spices, dressings, beverages
- **Other items:** crystals, figurines, key chains, seashells, sea glass, art projects, craft projects

TAKE YOUR TREASURES TO THE NEXT LEVEL

At first, you will simply gather and decide on your treasured items, and over time you will get more comfortable presenting your treasures in an ASMR session. After that, you will be looking for your next challenge. The last chapters in the book will explain how you can turn many of your treasured items into role-plays. With creativity, imagination, acting, and perhaps some fun costumes, role-plays will help you take your treasures to the next level.

CHAPTER 8
ASSUAGING ACTIVITIES

FOUNDATIONS OF ASSUAGING ACTIVITIES

Observing someone perform activities like painting, drawing, solving a puzzle, applying makeup, brushing hair, using an electronic device, or creating origami can be a strong ASMR trigger. The individual performing is usually very skilled at the activity, although observing someone learn or practice an activity can also induce strong ASMR. The activity typically includes gentle speech or whispering as the person carefully and patiently guides the viewer through the activity. In fact, the foundations of activity-induced ASMR are almost the same as treasure-induced ASMR, the focus of Chapter 7. The key difference is that the focus is on a potentially valuable *skill* instead of a potentially valuable *object*.

The relaxation that viewers feel while observing these activities could be due to a couple of key factors:

1. If you can be focused on someone else who is focused on an activity, then that means you both are in a safe environment.
2. If the other person is taking the time to teach you a task, then that means he or she cares about you and is trying to help you. ASMR seems to commonly result from situations in which you feel safe and someone else is showing you that he or she cares about you in some way.

The most popular example of this type of ASMR trigger is Bob Ross. He was the host of the TV show *The Joy of Painting*, which first aired in the United States in the 1980s. Bob Ross is visually memorable for his curly hair, but it was his kind disposition and deft painting skills that brought the viewers to his canvas. Although his show preceded the awareness of ASMR, he is often referred to as "the Godfather of ASMR" because so many people have found his show soothing, relaxing, and tingle inducing.

Several aspects of his show highlight activity-induced ASMR:

- His caring disposition—he spoke softly and calmly.
- His methodology—he encouraged viewers not to worry about mistakes and often offered gentle suggestions rather than strict instructions for how to paint.
- The setting—he painted in a somewhat intimate single room while speaking casually to the viewers.
- The camera angles—the close-ups of his hands made viewers feel as if they were right there with him.
- The ASMR-inducing sounds that went along with his painting—tapping, brushing, and light scratching.

"I am sometimes triggered by watching someone perform an artistic task, like painting (e.g., Bob Ross) or calligraphy. It seems to be the meticulous, careful attention the person is giving to the task that stimulates ASMR. For instance, when watching someone write calligraphy, the careful, slow stroking of the pen (together with the sound it makes) would be the key to triggering my ASMR. When performing a task, go slowly, carefully, and rhythmically to induce ASMR."

—Karissa, 28, female, USA

Although Bob Ross would speak to and engage viewers, it was clear that his main focus was to create the painting. This is another major trait of activity-induced ASMR. The activities may have an element of personal attention, but it is the activity, not the viewer, that is the major focus.

The foundations of activity-induced ASMR include the following:

- Talent and knowledge of the activity
- A caring disposition
- Some personal attention
- A major focus on the activity
- An up-close view of the activity
- Some trigger sounds

The value of watching someone complete a task is information or learning how to complete a similar task. ASMR seems to be triggered in the presence of someone who not only shows immediate care for us but can also provide information helpful to our long-term survival.

Learning to paint may not be considered a life-or-death skill in our modern world, although it definitely provides food, shelter, and more for professional artists. Our brains did not evolve to learn specific skills but instead evolved to learn skills appropriate for a time and setting. A long time ago, watching someone build a fire could result in learning a useful skill. Today, watching someone defeat a top level in a video game can mesmerize us due to the performer's impressive skills.

Although talented individuals like Bob Ross are well known for inducing ASMR, being highly skilled at the activity may not be a necessary factor. Watching almost anyone paint carefully has the potential to stimulate ASMR. Even watching a focused child fill in a coloring book can stimulate ASMR. Being highly focused on the activity is a stronger asset than having a talent for the activity.

TRIGGER TIPS FOR ASSUAGING ACTIVITIES

Certain types of activities are better suited for triggering ASMR than others. Chances are you know how to do something—or want to learn something—that would be a good fit with ASMR.

SELECTING AN ACTIVITY

First, let's talk about what *not* to do. There are some types of activities that do not induce ASMR:

1. **Dangerous activities.** Feeling safe and comfortable is important for ASMR, so juggling sharp knives is not a good idea.
2. **Gross motor skills.** These are physical motions that involve large muscles and full-body movements like jumping, karate, break dancing, gymnastics, and push-ups. Although yoga is relaxing, teaching someone yoga probably won't induce ASMR because it involves gross motor skills.

The types of activities that *do* commonly induce ASMR involve fine motor skills. These are physical movements that use small muscles and small movements, like activities that require precise hand and finger coordination. Examples include knitting, drawing, origami, typing, and using a video game controller. Fine motor skills may be better at stimulating ASMR than gross motor skills because the demonstrations are more passive, and observing them is more intimate.

Your first challenge is to decide what suitable activity you will demonstrate in an ASMR session. If explaining treasured items to someone is like show-and-tell, then demonstrating an activity to someone is like a talent show. So begin by making a list of activities that you are especially skilled at, keeping your list focused on activities that mostly require the coordination of your hands and fingers. If you know how to apply makeup, then you can explain your techniques using a mannequin head or sheet of paper. Consult the "Trigger Toolbox" section in this chapter for ideas if you're stumped.

> **"I think the best technique to trigger ASMR in others who are observing is to love the task and to be yourself. I think being too self-aware is a bad thing in the case of stimulating ASMR."**
>
> —Stephanie, adviser to Whisperlodge
> and creator of BitterSuite, UK

Remember that many activities don't require talent per se but rather knowledge. Think of portable devices you know how to use and give a tutorial. Anything with knobs, buttons, or touch screens would work well.

Some activities, like silently reading a magazine, don't even require any special talent or knowledge. As long as you are deeply absorbed in the magazine, your focus, combined with the delightful sound of the pages turning, can be a great stimulator of ASMR.

PERFORMING THE ACTIVITY

Begin by sitting close to the other person, who should not be straining to see what you are doing. His or her view is as important as yours, so it should be as good. He or she should even be the same distance as you are from the activity you are performing with your hands. As mentioned in Chapter 7, the preferred distance for watching an ASMR activity is twelve inches (thirty centimeters). If you were solving a Rubik's Cube, this would be about the distance from your hands to your face.

Exhibit confidence when you start your demonstration. You will naturally be confident when demonstrating an activity that you have a lot of talent in, skill at, or knowledge about. That confidence can be helpful for triggering activity-induced ASMR. If you are demonstrating an activity that you don't have a lot of talent in or skill at, then you will probably lack confidence. One trick to use is to change your focus from demonstrating a talent or skill to demonstrating your style. Some people think Picasso and Pollock didn't have much talent, but everyone agrees they both had style. Regardless of how you draw or paint, that is your style—do it with confidence.

> **"In cases where the guest is watching me perform an activity on my own, it is important for me to be fully absorbed in it as well. My focus on the task at hand will encourage my guest to focus on it and on me too. Personal attention, whether on an object or on a person, is a very strong trigger for ASMR in my opinion."**
>
> —Melinda Lauw, cocreator of Whisperlodge, USA

Even more important than confidence is focus. You should be engrossed in the activity. This does not mean to ignore the other person; think of it as being focused mostly on the activity and partially on the viewer. Your first priority is to demonstrate the activity, so don't pause the activity to tell a story. The person should be getting entranced by your deep focus on the activity. Keep it engaging enough that the person feels like you genuinely want him or her to learn and understand what you are demonstrating. Just do it in a way that allows the other person to slide into a relaxed and zoned-out state.

NARRATING AN ACTIVITY

If you are new at performing the activity in front of other individuals or as part of an ASMR session, then you may feel nervous and awkward. Here are some tips to make your narration more natural for you and more relaxing for your viewer:

- First explain your intentions and actions, which will help the viewer understand what is about to happen. Being informed will help the other person relax.
- Communicate to the other person that you will be sitting close enough so he or she can see everything clearly.
- Encourage the viewer to zone out and just passively absorb your actions and words.

"A specific example is watching a child play— the aspects that triggered ASMR were explaining what he was doing, doing the task repetitively, and speaking in a soft voice. Don't talk too much. If you do talk, leave gaps of not speaking, and explain what you are doing and why."

—Kristina, 44, female, USA

Encouraging the other person to zone out also reminds you to keep your words and actions focused to the activity. Try not to ask the other person questions. If you are explaining or teaching something, you might be tempted to say, "Is that clear?" or "Does that make sense?" or "Okay so far?" Remember that your major goal is to allow the person to passively observe, rather than actually teaching something. Also be careful about statements that might elicit a response. For example, the statement "I'm not sure if you have seen this done before, so I'll demonstrate it slowly" is not technically a question, but it can stimulate the other person to respond.

Be Caring

Even though you should be confident and focused, don't let that suppress your kind spirit. Share your tips, knowledge, skills, methods, and style as suggested techniques rather than as the best techniques for everyone. Bob Ross painted with confidence and focus, but his tender nature, encouraging words, and caring disposition always shone through. He allowed and encouraged mistakes. You can channel the spirit of Bob Ross or anyone in your life who explained something to you in a loving and caring way.

Volume and Pace

The volume of your voice should always be low, especially because you should be sitting very close to the other person. You can even allow the other person at the start to choose between soft vocals or whispering. Speak as if you are explaining the activity to yourself; that should keep you from projecting your voice too loudly. The pace of your words may be fast or slow, whichever way fits well with your enthusiasm, your focus, the activity, and the preference of the other person. Some individuals may enjoy nonstop rambling, and some may enjoy pauses while you think about something. You can try both and then ask for feedback after the session.

NOT NARRATING AN ACTIVITY

You don't actually have to say anything during the activity. A demonstration without vocals can be more engrossing than one with vocals because it focuses more attention on the activity than on what is being said. Sitting with someone without speaking is sometimes the ultimate expression of comfort and intimacy. It may feel awkward at first, but you both will quickly settle into a quiet and comfortable zone.

Another benefit to not speaking is it allows the other person to focus on any trigger sounds. One activity that stimulates ASMR in a lot of individuals is sitting next to another person who is silently reading a magazine. The focus of the reader, combined with the turning and crinkling of the pages, is great at stimulating ASMR. At the start of any silent activity, encourage the other person to focus on the sounds of whatever you are doing; this will also help remove the focus from the potentially awkward silence.

Selecting activities with trigger sounds is a great strategy if you're not going to narrate. A 2017 *PeerJ* research study reported that twice as many individuals who experience ASMR would rather watch someone fold paper into origami than watch someone fold towels. Paper folding may have been preferred because it contains a visual activity and the trigger sounds of paper, whereas towel folding only contains a visual activity. Be careful not to assume what the other person will like the most, though. Someone may not like paper crinkling and therefore may prefer towel folding with some whispering added. Always try to tailor an activity to an individual rather than just doing what is popular with most people.

TRIGGER TOOLBOX FOR ASSUAGING ACTIVITIES

Now that you know how to set up an activity session, it's time to think about what you'd actually do. Again, the keys are to be confident, focused, and caring about what you're explaining. The more comfortable you feel performing the activity, the more relaxed your viewer will be.

PAINTING

Material Options

- Paint types
- Paintbrush types
- Surface types

Activity Options

- Demonstrate your artistic talent or just paint with your own style.
- Paint with water-based or oil-based paint on canvas, canvas board, fiberboard, wood, cardboard, or paper as a surface.
- Create trigger sounds by using painting tools to apply paint by tapping, dabbing, swiping, brushing, scraping, spreading, and wiping. You can also create trigger sounds by mixing paint on a palette with a palette knife and handling bundles of paintbrushes.

DRAWING AND WRITING

Material Options

- Writing utensils
- Surface types

Activity Options

- Draw shapes, characters, or sketches or illustrate your life story or another story on blank paper with pens, pencils, or markers.
- Write a letter in calligraphy or cursive on lined paper.
- Design a house, garden, maze, or battle plan on graph paper.

- Trace scenes from a comic book, catalog, or holiday card on tracing paper. Use thin tracing paper for light crinkling sounds or thicker paper for deeper crinkling sounds.
- Create trigger sounds by adjusting the paper often, erasing marks, and then swiping or blowing away the eraser particles and frequently rummaging through a pile of drawing implements as you repeatedly switch utensils.

COLORING

Material Options

- Coloring utensils
- Coloring book types

Activity Options

- Use colored pencils, crayons, or markers with a traditional children's coloring book, an educational coloring book, or an adult coloring book. Educational coloring books cover many topics, including the solar system, human anatomy, geography, animals, languages, and history. Adult coloring books have much more intricate and complex designs and are reported to reduce stress. Educational coloring books may be best for providing a topic to talk about, and adult coloring books may be best for a quiet and focused observation.
- Create trigger sounds by frequently switching colors so you can rummage through a pile or container of coloring utensils.

Pause Point

Download a free forty-five-page adult coloring book from this link: https://arttherapycoloring.com/freebie/.

SOLVING PUZZLES

Material Options

- Assembly puzzles
- Interlocking puzzles
- Mechanical puzzles

Activity Options

- Puzzles like Rubik's Cubes, twisting lock puzzles, and metal wire puzzles that you constantly manipulate in your hands are the most suitable and also can make terrific trigger sounds. Manipulating these puzzles silently can also allow the other person to better focus on the trigger sounds of the puzzle. These puzzles are referred to as assembly puzzles, interlocking puzzles, and mechanical puzzles.
- Be careful with puzzles. The other person may become interested in helping you solve the puzzle, which will excite his or her brain and may inhibit ASMR. Puzzles that may not be good choices include word puzzles, tangram puzzles, peg puzzles, and sliding puzzles. Jigsaw puzzles also may not be a great idea because the person may start looking for pieces that fit together.

TABLETOP GAME TUTORIALS

Material Options

- Chess
- Checkers
- Dominoes
- Board games
- Card games

Activity Options

- These activities are likely to work best in a teaching session with soft vocals or whispering. Be careful about getting too focused on the vocal explanation without doing anything with your hands. Try to be continually touching, tapping, and handling game pieces and cards to enhance ASMR.
- Create trigger sounds by holding several plastic game pieces in one hand at a time, continually handling or shuffling cards, and creating subtle snap sounds with the corners of cards as you place them down on the table.
- After initially explaining a solitaire card game, this type of game may work well to do silently while the other person watches you.

MAGIC TRICKS

Material Options

- Card tricks
- Coin tricks
- Other magic tricks

Activity Options

Magic tricks can be ideal for ASMR sessions because they usually involve precise hand movements, handling of items, and soothing voices. It is interesting to wonder if the relaxing triggers of magic acts decrease the ability of viewers to notice the trick. You can perform tricks with narration, perform them silently, or explain them as tutorials.

READING OR BROWSING

Material Options

- Magazines
- Catalogs
- Newspapers
- Children's books
- Religious texts
- Phone books

> **"Sorting through cards and shuffling is a good technique, or you could perform a mundane task such as typing, reading a book, page turning, or writing. Watching someone perform a task can trigger my ASMR if he or she is whispering too. Inaudible whispers and tracing fingers over pages in a book triggers me."**
>
> —Holly ASMR, *YouTube* artist, UK

Activity Options

- Reading or browsing are great activities to perform for individuals who enjoy paper crinkling. The materials can be read word for word, browsed with commentary, or browsed silently.
- Materials that have words with pictures, like magazines, catalogs, and children's books, have some extra benefits. The text allows for word-for-word reading, and the pictures allow for additional commentary. Even more beneficial is that the pictures allow for constant touching, tracing, and tapping on.

- Materials like religious texts and phone books tend to have very thin pages and can make gentle and soothing crinkling sounds.
- Materials without pictures can provide a less distracting experience, and you can still use your hands by sliding your finger along the text as you read.

DEVICE DEMONSTRATIONS

Material Options

- Phones
- Tablets
- Calculators
- Cameras
- Camcorders
- Portable recorders

Activity Options

- Small devices with touch screens, buttons, switches, and knobs that you can hold in your hand can work great to stimulate ASMR.
- For mobile devices, you can explain the settings and options of the operating system or demonstrate some of your favorite apps. Make sure to select settings and apps that involve a lot of constant screen touching and swiping.
- For other devices, begin by displaying all sides with touching and tapping and then continue to explain the purpose of each button, knob, or switch, along with any screen menus. Keep explanations of each function or screen brief so you are constantly touching the device in some way.

VIDEO GAME DEMONSTRATIONS

Material Options

- Console games
- Computer games
- Mobile app games
- Handheld games

Activity Options

- Most of the popularity of watching online gaming is probably due to the excitement of watching someone else excel at a familiar game. (Always be cautious not to get too excited when playing a game. Treat it as a calm tutorial rather than a high-energy exhibition.) This means that you should pick games that the other person is not familiar with so he or she is focused on your expertise rather than your techniques and strategies.
- Console games with hand controllers have the extra benefit of complex hand movements and trigger sounds.
- Touch-screen games and handheld games also benefit from constant hand and finger movements.
- Surprisingly, even computer games with just a mouse controller can be very relaxing, especially with some soothing narration.

SOFTWARE DEMONSTRATIONS

Material Options

- Software and online programs for word processing
- Spreadsheets
- Presentations
- Audio or video editing
- Cloud storage
- Social media sites or tools

Activity Options

- It is likely that you have some programs that you use frequently and can explain well. These programs tend to have lots of menus to click through and explain. When demonstrating on a computer rather than a touch-screen device, try to incorporate a mix of trigger sounds such as mouse clicks, touch-pad swipes and clicks, and keyboard typing. If you are using a mouse, then try to gesture to items on the screen with your finger rather than your cursor.
- Try to create a constant and steady mix of vocals, hand movements, and trigger sounds to provide the best multi-sensory experience.

"Watching someone typing on the keyboard and doing office work triggers my ASMR a lot."

—Tony Bomboni, *YouTube* artist, USA

MAKEUP APPLICATION

Material Options

- Lipsticks
- Eye shadows
- Eyeliners
- Blushes
- Lip glosses
- Lip balms

Activity Options

- For observation-triggered ASMR, you will be applying the makeup to yourself or a mannequin head rather than the other person. If you have a third person available, then you could also apply the makeup to that individual.

- Makeup demonstrations are terrific opportunities to combine tranquil treasures and assuaging activities. You can begin by displaying and explaining the large selection of makeup products you own, then proceed to select one and apply it.
- Incorporate trigger sounds by handling several products at once, tapping on items, and removing caps and lids repeatedly.

HAND CARE

Material Options

- Nail files
- Nail buffers
- Nail polish
- Nail polish remover
- Cuticle oil
- Hand lotion

Activity Options

- As with the process of applying makeup, you will be providing hand care to yourself, a fake hand, or a third person, rather than the other participant.
- Be careful of the fumes associated with nail polish application and removal; the unhealthy fumes can create an alert response and may inhibit ASMR. To avoid fumes, you could purchase empty nail polish bottles and fill them with water just to demonstrate the motions of applying nail polish. You can also purchase nontoxic nail polishes that tend to be water based, odor-free, and sometimes marketed as organic or child friendly. These nontoxic polishes can be removed with rubbing alcohol rather than acetone.

HAIR CARE

Material Options

- Hairbrushes
- Hair styling tools
- Hair accessories
- Scissors
- Shampoo

Activity Options

- As with makeup application and hand care, you can provide hair care to yourself, a mannequin head, or a third person, rather than the other participant.
- Brushing and styling hair may be the easiest activities to demonstrate on yourself. Style your hair with mousse, lotion, or gel, rather than noxious hair sprays. As an alternative to hair spray, you can fill a trigger spray bottle with water, which would also provide gentle spritzing sounds.
- Rummage through, handle, tap on, or utilize hair accessories like clips, barrettes, combs, picks, pins, and rollers for additional trigger sounds.

ADDITIONAL ACTIVITY IDEAS

The following are other ideas for activities with soothing ASMR potential:

- Fold paper (origami)
- Fold towels
- Demonstrate food preparation and cooking
- Build structures with LEGOs
- Explain tarot cards
- Make and demonstrate slime

- Tend a mini Zen garden
- Trim a bonsai tree
- Demonstrate kinetic sand
- Demonstrate knitting techniques

TAKE YOUR ACTIVITIES TO THE NEXT LEVEL

As you can take your treasures to the next level, you can also take your activities to the next level. Over time you will become great at performing assuaging activities in your ASMR sessions, and then you might be looking to kick it up a notch. Part 3 will explain how you can combine your activities from this chapter with a script, an imaginary setting, and creative costumes to turn them into role-plays.

PART 3
RELAXING ROLE-PLAY SCENARIOS

What else can you do with your toolbox of hundreds of trigger ideas? Perform role-plays! Role-plays are usually reenactments of real situations, including the actions and personas that commonly trigger ASMR. Fictional or fantasy scenarios can also provide the basis for a role-play. The person stimulating the ASMR usually speaks, and the other person may remain silent or reply minimally. Costumes and props can be included to add more realism or fun.

These next chapters about role-plays won't introduce you to any new ASMR triggers. To create a role-play, you will be incorporating all those tips, techniques, and tools you already learned in Part 2, and then add a setting, storyline, script, characters, costumes, and props to create a role-play. Some fine acting skills and creative energy will meld it all together into an immersive and tingly production.

Chapter 9 focuses on role-plays involving touch and Chapter 10 focuses on role-plays that don't involve touch. These two types of role-plays involve different perspectives, techniques, scenarios, and other important considerations that will be discussed in each chapter. Some tips and techniques apply to both types, such as: how should you prepare for a role-play?

- Start with visualizing your own relaxing experiences, like getting an eye exam or a makeup consultation. Your own memories and experiences will be the easiest for you to create and reenact as role-plays.
- View ASMR videos for inspiration of style and ideas for adding trigger sounds.
- Consult in-depth and reputable online resources about your particular topic. This will help you to blend in realism and knowledge.
- And finally, try to get real experience in the activity if you don't have any. If you are doing a manicure role-play and you have never had a manicure, go treat yourself in the name of research.

How should you prepare the setting?

- Identify the exact space you will perform the role-play in and arrange the furniture appropriately.
- Make sure you can move around the space adequately and it is comfortable for the other person.
- Gather your props and outfit, then test those in the space to make sure there are no unexpected problems like your outfit snagging on the arm of a chair every time you walk behind it.

How should you create your action plan?

- Jot down the general actions you will perform in the role-play.
- Decide where each of you will be at the start of the role-play, the procedures you will perform, and your general time line.
- Add a basic script to your action plan by inserting statements that you will say during your role-play.
- At a minimum, your script should begin with a greeting, continue with an explanation of what you are going to do, and a have concluding statement to let the other person know the role-play has ended.

Following are some helpful tips for creating a script:

- Create a general outline of what you want to say during your role-play. You don't want your outline to be overly detailed, or it will be too difficult to remember.
- If you are too scripted and robotic with your words and actions, then the other person is less likely to experience ASMR. You should sound real and genuine.
- Therefore, most of your role-play should be improvisational. Winging it and making up stuff as you go will make the scenario more natural, enjoyable, and relaxing for both of you.

You may not think of yourself as an actor, but then you put on some type of costume or outfit, and the transformation happens naturally. After you have created and successfully performed your first role-play, you will probably find yourself excited to create your next one. Get new costumes on sale after Halloween and other holidays. Visit thrift stores and browse the clothing and wares for additional outfits and props.

Role-plays can be a wonderful challenge and outlet for creative individuals and lead to increased interest in your ASMR sessions. Someone may not leave your session and tell his or her friends how good you are at turning magazine pages, but high-production role-plays may establish your ASMR sessions as the most talked about in your area. Be creative, have fun, induce tingles.

CHAPTER 9
HANDS-ON ROLE-PLAYS

FOUNDATIONS OF HANDS-ON ROLE-PLAYS

Role-plays are hands on if any type of touching is involved, such as with hands or with objects like a hairbrush or a stethoscope. Examples of hands-on role-plays include getting a simulated haircut from a hairdresser or receiving a physical exam from someone acting as a clinician.

The advantage of hands-on role-plays, as opposed to hands-off ones, is the potential benefit of touch. The inclusion of light touch with personal attention and gentle vocals in a realistic enactment can stimulate strong ASMR. The disadvantage of hands-on role-plays is that you may not feel comfortable touching the other person or vice versa. This chapter will focus on hands-on role-plays, and the next chapter will focus on hands-off role-plays so that you can gather information about both types.

Chapter 5 (Feathery Fingers) introduced you to the foundations of touching someone with your hands to stimulate ASMR. Those same foundations apply here because some of these hands-on role-plays will involve you touching the other person with your hands. Similarly, Chapter 6 (Tingly Tools) introduced you to the foundations of touching someone with objects to stimulate ASMR. The same foundations in that chapter will also apply here because you may be touching the other person with props that are part of the role-play.

> **"It's really important that role-playing comes across as natural and realistic as possible. When we received tingles early in life before videos dedicated to inducing the feeling came along, we were triggered by natural sounds, and I think the experience is intensified the closer to an everyday situation it is."**
>
> —Amanda, WhisperSparkles ASMR, *YouTube* artist, UK

In those two prior chapters that focused on touch, the major focus was the light touch and the minor focus was the personal attention. The person being touched could close his or her eyes and focus mostly on the touch. In this chapter, the major focus is the personal attention and the light touch has the minor role. This is an important distinction. During a hands-on role-play, the other person should always—or at least often—be aware and focused on your presence and your touch. He or she should feel the strong spotlight of your attention and the light pressure of your touch.

Pause Point

You can begin your exploration into role-plays by enjoying a playlist of more than fifty ASMR role-play videos by Emma WhispersRed: www.youtube.com/playlist?list=PLWk4fkmkuf3vEMNt PW90yGPo13dDsLedX, and a playlist of more than thirty role-play videos by Dr Dmitri (MassageASMR): www.youtube.com/ playlist?list=PL1OPyJWm858Jyn_EkJr5rjv1uin1MUvQ3.

Some of the most popular ASMR videos are role-plays that incorporate simulated touching, like a visit with a doctor or makeup specialist. Therefore, your in-person role-plays are also likely to be very popular. You may even want to specialize in one type of hands-on role-play. For example, specializing in clinical role-plays could mean writing a variety of scripts based on clinical procedures, gathering a large selection of real or fake medical instruments, accumulating a wardrobe of various medical uniforms, and building a space for your sessions that replicates a medical office. Or maybe you specialize in spa role-plays, hairdresser role-plays, or alien abduction role-plays.

> **"I find that for role-plays, the more familiar the guest is with the role-play character, the more effective it is. For example, a doctor role-play tends to be more effective than a fictional, fantastical character role-play. This is probably because the guest won't have to spend extra effort understanding the relationship dynamic and can easily sink into focusing on the triggers themselves. That being said, I think this is incredibly subjective too. I'm a fan of fictional role-play ASMR videos."**
>
> —Melinda Lauw, cocreator of Whisperlodge, USA

TRIGGER TIPS FOR HANDS-ON ROLE-PLAYS

Before we get into specific role-playing scenarios, let's review how to set up a session in a way that will maximize the potential for success.

GET CONSENT AND BE SANITARY

Begin your preparation for hands-on role-plays by reviewing all the trigger tips in Chapter 5 (Feathery Fingers). Almost all those tips apply to hands-on role-plays also—asking for consent before touching, knowing the appropriate areas for touching, encouraging the other person to wear clothing suitable for touching, washing your hands, and being aware of touch pressures and patterns.

Since you may be touching the other person with props in some of these role-plays, review all the trigger tips in Chapter 6 (Tingly Tools). These tips include testing all items for safety and sensation, properly cleaning the items, being aware of potential allergies, and explaining items before using them.

> **"My most frequently requested ASMR triggers involve 'personal attention' role-plays—videos in which I simulate the experience of tending to and focusing on the viewer. In these videos I act out scenarios such as giving the viewer a medical exam, spa treatment, or mystical energy healing. It's so common and normal for people to have an undersatiated craving for care and attention, and the simulated platonic intimacy these role-plays offer are an effective way for many people to partially fulfill that need."**
>
> —Jellybean Green, *YouTube* artist, USA

ROLE-PLAYS VERSUS REAL PROCEDURES

Clinical role-plays are a popular type of ASMR role-play. These role-plays usually involve someone acting like a professional clinician and simulating a medical procedure. Regardless of your medical training and knowledge, you *never* want to attempt real procedures. Keep any touching very light and don't try to reproduce the actual firmness of any physical examinations or manipulations. Some procedures have potential health risks, and you could directly harm the other person. You could also harm someone indirectly by performing a diagnostic test and giving him or her an incorrect diagnosis. Clarify at the start that you are performing simulated procedures that will not actually treat or diagnose the person.

Another popular type of ASMR role-play is beauty-care role-plays. These role-plays usually involve someone acting like an expert cosmetologist, beautician, or spa professional. There are some beauty procedures that should only be performed by trained professionals because they involve caustic chemicals or sharp instruments. On the other hand, there may be some actual beauty procedures that you both agree to including in a session because they don't involve chemicals or physical risk. Make sure to communicate clearly about what you will be doing and to get the other person's consent prior to beginning the session.

CLINICAL ROLE-PLAYS

Clinical role-plays are very popular as ASMR videos because real-life encounters with clinicians have great potential for stimulating ASMR. After all, clinical visits contain the following:

- Personal attention
- A caring disposition
- An expert in a field
- Light touch
- Fine motor skills
- Precision instruments
- Soothing speech

Clinical Props

One key prop to use in your clinical role-plays is a clipboard. This adds an air of professionalism; you can hide a script on it; you can crinkle, handle, and write on the paper as additional ASMR triggers; and it gives you something to do with your hands if you are nervous. Listening and taking notes are also great indirect ways to give someone personal attention, but don't always stare down at the clipboard because eye contact is very important in all role-plays.

Also, use latex-free medical gloves. They can put you and the other person in a medical state of mind, decrease hygiene concerns, and add delightful crinkly trigger sounds. If you are not using medical gloves, then you should wash or disinfect your hands immediately prior to the simulated medical procedure. One reason is that it is an actual thing all clinicians do—or at least should be doing—prior to touching a patient. Another reason is that you should be doing this anyway prior to any touch-mediated ASMR.

> **"My most requested role-play is the doctor role-play because I use materials such as latex gloves, which make tingly sounds when used correctly. Writing and making notes during the role-play is also relaxing, along with up-close whispering, face touching, and personal attention."**
>
> —Holly ASMR, *YouTube* artist, UK

Additional items like scrubs, a white coat, a stethoscope, and other clinical props can enhance a scenario, but you don't need them. Having the other person put on a medical gown that opens in the back is definitely not necessary, nor is it recommended.

Doing a clinical role-play is more about how you act than how you both look. Channel your lifetime of visits with clinicians into your best vision of a kind and caring health professional. Begin by asking how the other person is feeling. Then make eye contact, ask follow-up questions, listen carefully, take notes on a clipboard, and perform some type of simulated medical procedure.

Don't worry if you haven't memorized all the terminology and actual steps for a real medical procedure. You are not a medical professional, and the other person likely won't be either. Keep it simple. Use terms you know and then talk and act in a way that makes sense to you. It is okay to remain silent while performing a procedure—let your hands do the talking. Touch with your fingers, inspect with your eyes, ask simple questions, jot notes on a clipboard, repeat. Remember that this role-play is about touch and personal attention, so don't get lost in the scenario details.

BEAUTY-CARE ROLE-PLAYS

There is a good chance that you have experience providing some type of beauty care to yourself, so this type of role-play may be less intimidating than clinical role-plays. Like clinical role-plays, beauty-care role-plays are also very popular as ASMR videos because the typical aspects of beauty care include personal attention, someone providing care, a skilled expert, a light touch, and a professional talking to you in a calm voice.

> **"I love haircut role-plays because I am
> very sensitive to the sound of scissors. I
> love to feel a hand brushing my hair or a
> brush going slowly down my face."**
>
> —Paris ASMR, *YouTube* artist, France

Beauty-care role-plays can rely more on props than clinical role-plays. Making real or simulated changes to someone's hair, skin, hands, or fingernails will probably require specific tools. Make sure to plan out and practice a beauty role-play to confirm you have the tools you need. As with clinical procedures, it is okay to remain silent while providing care—allow your hands to do the talking. You can also provide professional beauty tips or make small talk, but remember to keep the attention focused on the other person by asking questions and listening carefully.

Feel free to incorporate a clipboard into your beauty role-play for the same reasons you do in the clinical role-play.

TRIGGER TOOLBOX FOR HANDS-ON ROLE-PLAYS

Now, let's dive into specific suggestions for hands-on role-plays that might work for you and your recipients.

CLINICAL ROLE-PLAYS

The following role-plays have a medical theme.

Physical Exam

- **Real procedure:** A physical exam is a routine test usually performed to check someone's overall health status. It can also be called a clinical exam, an annual physical, a wellness exam, or a checkup. Typical procedures include checking vital signs (blood pressure, heart rate, breathing rate) and testing body parts for normal appearance, sensations, and functions. Blood tests may also be ordered to check the cells and chemicals in the blood.

- **Role-play:** You can begin the role-play by sitting face-to-face with the other person and asking about health concerns. Touching can be incorporated by feeling the pulse on his or her wrist, touching his or her back with a stethoscope or with your hand to assess breathing, examining skin for problems, touching in various areas to test sensory input, and manipulating joints to assess mobility. Basically, it is a general exam, so be creative and examine him or her in any way that allows you to touch gently and appropriately. Conclude the role-play with the encouragement of exercise, appropriate diet, and other healthy lifestyle choices.

Cranial Nerve Exam

- **Real procedure:** This is a neurological exam that investigates if the nerves connecting your brain to different parts of the head and neck are normal. The test may check all or most of the following: smell, taste, vision, hearing, eye movements, pupil reflex, facial nerves, chewing muscles, facial muscles, tongue movements, and neck muscles.
- **Role-play:** Cranial nerve exams are one of the most popular types of ASMR videos. The popularity is probably due to the diligent and focused attention to the head coupled with a variety of hand movements and light touching from a caring expert. Create a simulated cranial nerve exam by having the other person smell items, taste items, read eye charts or posters, follow your finger with eye movements, make facial expressions, open and close his or her jaw, and move his or her head. Touch your recipient's face lightly in various places with a tissue or swab to assess touch sensations. To prevent any potential damage to the retina, do not shine any light directly into the other person's eyes.

Ear Exam

- **Real procedure:** An ear exam is an inspection of the ear canal with a light to check for problems with the ear canal and eardrum.
- **Role-play:** First, do not insert anything into anyone's ear canal. Use your cell phone light or other light source to peek inside the ear canal while gently holding the outside of the ear. Focus your role-play on the outside of the ear. Take your time to touch and inspect the outside of the ears closely. Some individuals find ear inspections very relaxing.

Ear Cleaning

- **Real procedure:** Ear cleanings focus mostly on removing impacted wax or other debris from ear canals.
- **Role-play:** Do not attempt to clean anyone's ear canals by inserting an object or any type of fluid. Ear cleanings should only be attempted by medical professionals. Just focus your ear cleaning role-play on lightly touching the outside of the ear.

Eye Exam with Direct Inspection

- **Real procedure:** Eye exams assess vision, eye movements, pupil reflexes, and other aspects of eye health, and may include an eyeglasses fitting.
- **Role-play:** To prevent any potential damage to the retina, do not shine any light directly into the other person's eyes. You can assess vision by having him or her read an eye chart or poster and assess eye movements by moving your fingers

in specific ways. The touch aspect of this exam is the direct inspection of the eyes. To inspect the eyes, sit very close facing the other person and touch the facial skin under one lower eyelid very lightly without inhibiting his or her ability to blink. Instruct the other person to look in different directions and to continue blinking normally while you inspect each eye. Use his or her real eyeglasses or frames without lenses to pretend to fit him or her for glasses. Touch and adjust the frames to sit properly on his or her face.

> **"When I was a teenager, I loved going to the optometrist! She had a wonderful and soothing voice, and the way she enunciated the letters *T*, *P*, and *S* triggered a lot of tingles! She would also touch me around the eyes when examining my eyes or adjusting the eyeglasses I was trying on."**
>
> —Somni Rosae, *YouTube* artist, Canada

Head Lice Exam

- **Real procedure:** A head lice exam is performed by inspecting someone's hair and scalp for adult lice and their eggs. Inspection is done by parting the hair in different places directly with hands or with the aid of a comb. A special fine-tooth comb is used to remove the lice eggs.
- **Role-play:** Use your fingers with or without a comb to thoroughly inspect the hair and entire scalp. Visualize nature documentaries that show monkeys or apes grooming each other. The role-play can be done as a simple diagnostic inspection so you don't necessarily need to find lice; just

spend lots of time looking to be thorough…and to induce tingles.

> **"The head lice check from elementary school, with the chopsticks (or whatever they used) tracing your scalp always triggered my ASMR."**
>
> —Kim, 39, female, Canada

Cranial Phrenology Exam

- **Real procedure:** This procedure is not used by medical professionals and is not considered diagnostic or meaningful. It is an ancient procedure that relates bumps on someone's head to his or her personality or health.
- **Role-play:** Gently guide your fingers over the person's scalp to assess the bumps and dips of his or her skull. You can act like it is a diagnostic test and inform the person about his or her health or act like it is a personality test and inform the person about his or her disposition and character. You can also act like it is a horoscope and inform him or her about the future. Be creative and have fun.

Hand Exam

- **Real procedure:** A hand exam is a thorough examination of someone's hand for disorders of the skin, vessels, nerves, muscles, anatomy, and functionality. There is a wide range of tests and procedures that can be done depending on the potential disorder.
- **Role-play:** Inspect the surface of the person's hands for skin or vessel disorders. Trace and lightly touch blood vessels to assess vascular health. Gently squeeze fingers, knuckles, wrists, and

hand bones to assess bone health. Ask the person to move his or her hands and fingers in various ways to evaluate nerve and muscle functionality. Have him or her perform subtle wrist movements to test for carpal tunnel syndrome. Have him or her lightly press on your hands and fingers in various ways to assess strength and potential pain disorders.

Skin Exam

- **Real procedure:** A skin exam involves inspection of the skin for benign or cancerous growths, swollen lymph nodes, blemishes, cysts, small wounds, and lesions. A detailed inspection may be done with a dermatoscope, which provides magnification and light.
- **Role-play:** Inspect general skin areas for moles and other surface anomalies. Inspect the facial area for healthy follicles and pores. Touch on or around areas of interest for raised surfaces. You can use the camera on your cell phone as a simulated dermatoscope for specific areas of interest. Use the zoom function to magnify the skin; switching to the video function should allow you to zoom and have your light on at the same time.

BEAUTY-CARE ROLE-PLAYS

Following are some options for relaxing beauty role-plays.

Haircuts Using Scissors

- **Real procedure:** A hairstylist uses scissors to cut someone's hair.
- **Role-play:** You can simulate a haircut by touching a person's hair with one hand and snapping the scissors open and

closed with the other. You will not actually cut the hair, of course, and you will want to remain focused for safety reasons. Incorporate spray bottles with water for spritz sounds around the head or use empty spray bottles for light air puffs on the scalp and neck. Use smaller scissors to create different sounds, for simulated trimming around the ears, and for mustaches and beards.

Haircuts and Shaves Using Clippers

- **Real procedure:** A hairstylist uses electric clippers to cut someone's hair.
- **Role-play:** Touch the person's hair with one hand, a comb, or a hair pick to provide the feel of a razor and move the razor around with the other to provide the sound. You will not actually touch the razor to the person's skin, of course, and you will want to remain focused for safety reasons. Simulated shaving of the neck and face can be done by putting a thick guard comb on an electric razor so the cutting edge does not reach the skin or any hair. Simulate electric shaving of hair on ears by touching the backside of a small electric shaver to the outer perimeter of the ear.

Face and Neck Shave

- **Real procedure:** A person using shaving cream with a safety razor or straight edge razor to shave facial and neck hair.
- **Role-play:** Begin by applying a warm towel to the area to be shaved to "soften the hairs." Dab on a little bit of facial lotion and massage it in to "lubricate the hairs." Apply a small amount shaving cream to face and neck and then remove gently with an object that isn't sharp, like a popsicle

stick or the back of a comb. Use slow and steady strokes in the direction of the hair growth to be authentic or in the opposite direction if there's too much resistance. End with another warm towel to "help the follicles settle back to a relaxed state."

Hairstyling

- **Real procedure:** Hairstyling usually involves the cutting, drying, and styling of hair with the addition of liquid-based substances or hair accessories to hold the style in place.
- **Role-play:** You can incorporate simulated cutting or just focus on the styling. The "Trigger Toolbox" section in Chapter 5 has a long list of options for hair accessories, hair-shaping substances, and examples of hair braids, updos, and buns. To create a hairstyling role-play, combine the specific methods and techniques for hairstyling from Chapter 5 with the simulated setting and behaviors of a hair salon.

Pause Point

The 2017 movie *Battle of the Sexes* is about the historical tennis match between Billie Jean King (played by Emma Stone) and Bobby Riggs (played by Steve Carell). It was also the first major motion picture to have a scene that was intentionally created to induce ASMR. The movie directors studied ASMR recordings and designed the hair salon scene to be delightfully relaxing. The scene accentuated the soothing mannerisms of the hairdresser, such as gentle hair touching, nurturing hand movements, light whispering, soft vocalizing, and hypnotic scissor snipping.

Makeup Application

- **Real procedure:** Makeup is applied to a male or female to enhance or alter facial features for personal appearance, a stage or film performance, a costume, face painting, or cosplay. Common makeup options include lipsticks, eye shadows, eyeliners, blushes, and foundations, along with additional options for costumes and special effects.
- **Role-play:** You can apply real makeup if the other person agrees to it. The role-play then becomes the setting or reason for the makeup, like a stage performance, identity change, costume, first date, wedding, or just simply visiting a cosmetologist. Face paints can be used for easy removal. You can also pretend to apply makeup as a role-play. Makeup types that are normally applied with brushes are the easiest to fake and work wonderfully to stimulate ASMR. Makeup pencils and liners can be simulated with chopsticks or other blunt instruments, but always be careful around the eyes.

Hand and Nail Care

- **Real procedure:** Hand and fingernail care can include hand lotion, cuticle oil, top and base coats, cuticle nipping and pushing, nail polish, nail filing, nail sanding and buffing, nail art, nail cleaning, and nail accessories.
- **Role-play:** As with applying real makeup, the other person may desire you to provide some type of real nail care. As mentioned in Chapter 8 (Assuaging Activities), be careful of the fumes associated with nail polish application and removal because they can create an alert response and inhibit ASMR. You can also purchase nontoxic nail polishes, which may be labeled as water based, odor-free, organic, or child friendly. You can also simulate the application of nail polish

by purchasing empty nail polish bottles and filling them with water.

Tattoo Applications

- **Real procedure:** A tattoo artist uses a needle to insert ink into the skin in an artistic pattern or image.
- **Role-play:** For safety purposes, do not attempt to do real tattoos or incorporate real needles into a role-play. Instead, you can simply pretend to draw on someone's skin or use special markers created for drawing on someone's skin. Markers that are washable and nontoxic that would work well for drawing fake tattoos are called body art pens, body markers, skin markers, tattoo pens, and temporary tattoo pens; even face-paint crayons could be used.

Pause Point

Other ideas for hands-on role-plays include eyebrow threading, henna hand art, palm reading, clothing fitting, and ring fitting.

NEXT-LEVEL ROLE-PLAYS

Most of the role-plays suggested here are simple and direct simulations of real and common scenarios. You can be a lot more creative and inventive. How about doing some hands-on role-plays as a crime scene investigator, sci-fi suit repair person, fairy godmother, or Hunger Games tribute makeover artist? To view all of these as actual role-plays and much more, check out this playlist of more than seventy video ASMR role-plays (hands on and hands off) from Heather Feather: www.youtube.com/playlist?list=PLHFqg6zxO2CFrYSm2wpQQI4enqXraAs04.

CHAPTER 10
HANDS-OFF ROLE-PLAYS

FOUNDATIONS OF HANDS-OFF ROLE-PLAYS

Hands-off role-plays can include any trigger type except touch. This chapter focuses on hands-off role-plays because there may be times when it is not appropriate or desired to incorporate touch into an ASMR session. It could simply be your preference, or it could be the preference of the other person. Individuals who don't like being touched may also prefer more personal space, another consideration for hands-off role-plays. Having the awareness, option, and boundaries of hands-off role-plays is something you and the other person will probably appreciate at some point.

Even though hands-off role-play won't have you physically interacting with the other person, these role-plays should still be very engaging—you will just be engaging him or her with focused attention and perhaps dialogue. ASMR videos with interview, survey, or question scenarios are popular hands-off role-plays. The person asking the questions always has a kind disposition and is usually sitting behind a desk, which provides ample personal space for the other person. The questions are never tough or stress inducing and are usually asked with genuine curiosity and interest.

Another type of hands-off role-play in some ASMR videos is consultation, sales, or demonstration scenarios. These scenarios may involve someone standing behind a counter or sitting at a table with items in front of him or her. The counter or table provides a subtle boundary to give the viewer a feeling of appropriate personal space. The items are handled amply and displayed to the viewer along with explanations or sometimes questions. As per most hands-off role-plays, these scenarios include a caring personality, personal attention, item touching, trigger sounds, and sometimes lightly engaging questions.

> "My favorite type of role-plays are teacher role-plays where the person is talking through a topic, sharing knowledge, information, and visual stimulants such as images or letters traced while they talk. I really enjoy shopping channel role-plays because they are calm and slow and show things to talk about—they combine sounds with talking. Talk a lot and do things like showing other items and writing on boards as an addition to talking. Using a pointer to trace or outline the words is a good technique if reading from something. Take your time and be patient."
>
> —Imperfect ASMR, *YouTube* artist, UK

TRIGGER TIPS FOR HANDS-OFF ROLE-PLAYS

The following tips will help you create role-plays that are reasonable for you to act out and relaxing for your recipient.

GETTING IDEAS AND MAKING A SCRIPT

Review the tips for hands-on role-plays in the Part 3 introduction because some of them also apply to hands-off role-plays. For example, think of your own experiences to brainstorm a scenario, watch ASMR videos to get ideas, and consult factual resources related to your role-play to make your setup realistic. Identify and test the area for your role-play for appropriateness and safety.

Then you can outline the actions that will occur during the role-play and add a suitable script. Remember not to overscript or overact your role-play. Being genuine and natural will result in the most relaxing role-play for the other person.

FINDING PROPS

Specific props may vary from scenario to scenario, but there are a few items that will be helpful in almost any case.

Clipboard

The clipboard was mentioned as a helpful prop in hands-on role-plays, and it is also helpful for hands-off role-plays involving surveys, interviews, and forms. Revisit the prior chapter to review the specific benefits and techniques for using a clipboard in a role-play.

Name Badge

In every hands-off role-play, you will be assuming a different profession. You may be a researcher, employer, pharmacist, beautician, motivational counselor, or salesperson. Each of your identities should have a name to further focus you in a role-play. Therefore, a simple prop to add to all these role-plays is a name badge. Purchase the type of name badge that allows you to slide a piece of paper into a plastic sleeve; this will allow you to easily swap out different pieces of paper for each role-play. Look for the type that can be pinned to your shirt or worn on a lanyard to give you some variety in how you wear it.

Handheld Pointer

Another wonderful prop for most hands-off role-plays is a handheld pointer. This is any long, thin item you can hold in your hand to tap on items or gesture toward them. There are several advantages to using a pointer instead of your fingers and hands. As with a clipboard, it adds some flair of expertise and gives you something to hold if you have nervous hands. A pointer can also add a distinctive and subtle *tap* sound when you touch some items. Additionally, some individuals who don't like being touched may have a conscious or subconscious preference that you use a pointer rather than your hands to touch nearby items.

Professional pointers are usually sold as wooden pointers, teacher pointers, hand pointers, or classroom pointers. Pointers that can extend and collapse may have the additional keywords *telescoping, flagpole, collapsible*, or *extending*. As an alternative, you could also use a small antenna, a selfie stick, a plastic magic wand, a ruler, a wooden kitchen utensil (hold it backward), or a chopstick, or simply walk outside and pick a suitable stick off the ground.

ESTABLISHING PERSONAL SPACE

If someone has requested not to be touched, then he or she may also be uncomfortable with others being too close. Ask the person what distance is most comfortable. Many hands-off role-plays may already involve a desk or table that would be between you and the other person. If the role-play does not naturally involve a physical buffer between you and the other person, then try adding one. As an alternative, simply sitting a bit farther away may work well enough. As always, the important thing is to be aware of potential personal space preferences and to do your best to make the other person comfortable and relaxed.

MANAGING SOUND

If you are sitting behind a large desk or table, the other person might not be able to hear your whispers or mouth sounds very well. You may not anticipate this because you can always hear the whispers and mouth sounds of your favorite video artist when he or she is behind a desk.

Be sure to test out your setting with someone else to determine how well you can be heard. Using a smaller table or desk or talking in a soft voice rather than a whisper may help. If you are determined to deliver gentle whispers and subtle mouth sounds from a distance, you could use a microphone, and the other person could wear headphones. Your microphone would plug into the audio input of a recording device, and the headphones would plug into the audio output of the same device. Set the recorder to record or to monitor without recording, and your subtle sounds should then pass directly into the ears of the other person.

DETERMINING LEVELS OF ENGAGEMENT

ASMR videos that include interview or consultation scenarios usually have the person in the video asking questions of the viewer. Some are simple yes-or-no questions, and some require more in-depth responses. This is relaxing to the viewer because it is strong personal attention without any pressure or brain energy required to actually respond. If you ask someone similar questions in an in-person scenario, then that person probably will respond, which may not be as relaxing for him or her. This is an important distinction between being asked a question by someone in a video and being asked a question by someone in real life. Actually answering those simple or open-ended questions may not seem like a big deal, but the other person's brain has to become more active to answer. He or she may find that answering the questions is less relaxing because it feels silly, personal, difficult, or he or she is trying to come up with an answer that pleases, impresses, or amuses you. Answering questions may therefore overly engage or stress some individuals and decrease their ASMR.

> **"Interviews are not as much of a trigger for me, nor is anything that involves a reaction or an implied decision because it's engaging a different mental energy, the one I am trying to rest from. When it comes to ASMR, I want to be talked to, not with. The most relaxing role-plays for ASMR purposes, in my opinion, are those where the artist sits in one place for the duration and all movement has a flow to it."**
>
> —Kim, 39, female, Canada

You can try modifying your question-and-answer scenarios to decrease potential stress. One option is to make sure you only ask yes-or-no questions; that takes a lot of stress out of replying. You could tell the person not to answer your questions because you're role-playing a content creator in an ASMR video, and he or she is pretending to be at home viewing the video—how deeply meta. You could also have the person complete a form before the role-play or pretend that he or she already completed a form so your role-play is you commenting on all the replies by looking over a completed form or survey.

This does not mean that you should never ask open-ended questions. It could turn out that some individuals have a stronger ASMR response by answering in-person questions because it is genuine engagement and attention. If the other person wants to answer questions, then make sure to give him or her the option of providing real or creative replies. The important perspective is awareness of this variety of responses and the options you can try. Try different types of engagement and then ask the person after one or more sessions which method he or she found the most relaxing.

Q&A ROLE-PLAYS

Q&A role-plays basically involve you asking the other person questions. Asking questions in a gentle and interested way can elicit a strong feeling of personal attention. The questions may be part of a role-play about a job application, a teacher evaluation, a personality quiz, or completing a medical history. Be careful about asking any questions about personal, private, or sensitive topics. Always give the person the option of skipping a question or making something up.

Pause Point

Access hundreds of form templates for your role-plays at this site: www.jotform.com/form-templates/.

You can find many real forms, sample forms, and template forms online to help you create your role-plays. You can print the forms out and then write down the replies to add paper and writing trigger sounds. Alternately, you can use electronic versions of the forms and type in the replies on a keyboard to add typing trigger sounds. Don't worry if you can't get an electronic version that allows you to type into it. As long as you have a list of questions somewhere, you can just type the replies into any blank document or just make typing sounds and not actually record the replies.

You don't even have to record (or pretend to record) the replies at all. You could simply sit back, ask the questions, and listen to the replies. This can provide more of a face-to-face, personal interaction. This also allows you to provide more eye contact, really listen to the replies, and follow up with questions that may not be in front of you. The result can be a more engaging, casual, and genuine role-play. Job interviews are naturally like this, but you could use this format for many of the Q&A role-plays.

CONSULTATION ROLE-PLAYS

Consultation role-plays basically involve the other person coming to you for your assistance. You could be providing that person with an eye exam, filling a prescription, providing beauty tips, guiding him or her into a relaxation state, motivating him or her to achieve a goal, or helping him or her understand a problem. Some of these role-plays may involve medical or mental health topics. Make sure the other person knows that anything you say during a role-play should not replace or deter actual assistance from a real professional.

The optometrist and pharmacist scenarios will be more realistic if you both are standing up. However, it may be better to do these scenarios with you both sitting down to make them more relaxing. The other scenarios naturally work well with you both sitting down and facing each other. Make ample eye contact, listen carefully, and offer genuine assistance. Wearing appropriate clothing to the type of role-play can assist you in feeling more natural.

SALES ROLE-PLAYS

Sales role-plays are mostly about selling items but also include some demonstration and tasting. You will usually be acting as a store employee or a sales representative. The common theme in most of these role-plays is that you are trying to convince the other person that a specific product is an ideal fit for him or her. Confidence and expertise are part of being a good salesperson, and this can be a strong type of personal attention. Be careful, though, to be a caring consumer advocate rather than a pushy salesperson. Express genuine interest and effort in finding the best products for the other person.

How you set up the items for each role-play is important. Place chairs on opposite sides of a table and place the items on the table. The key part, though, is to place the items much closer to you. If you place them too close to the other person, then he or she will be inclined to pick them up. You need to be the one to pick up, touch, manipulate, and constantly handle the items to stimulate this type of ASMR. When the other person is holding the item instead of you, then his or her ASMR is on pause. It is okay to pass an item to him or her momentarily to keep the role-play realistic, but gently and kindly try to get it back into your hands quickly.

Another benefit of sales role-plays for stimulating ASMR is all the potential trigger sounds. The variety of role-plays and items allows for plastic crinkling, paper crinkling, mouth sounds, eating sounds, paper-turning sounds, lid-opening sounds, and a huge variety of tapping sounds due to all the different surfaces. Try not to get overly focused on formulating great sales pitches for each item; your real focus is providing personal attention, handling the items constantly, and creating lots of trigger sounds.

Some sales role-plays don't involve actual items but rather pictures of items and text. These role-plays involve catalogs, magazines, booklets, maps, brochures, and cookbooks. These role-plays may work better if you both are sitting on the same side of the table. Keep in mind that some individuals may prefer to have the table between you to ensure personal space. Tailor the seating arrangement to best fit the other person's preference for personal space.

> "My ASMR is primarily triggered from role-plays, so much so that I rarely seek out other content. My favorite types of role-plays are where the ASMRtist is in some kind of professional role: banker, travel agent, tailor, flight attendant, etc. Another role-play style I like is the instructional, though I see it rarely. From understanding Reiki to folding towels, it's a great way to get me focused on something visually, and the auditory tricks just take over."
>
> —Brandon, 32, male, USA

TRIGGER TOOLBOX FOR HANDS-OFF ROLE-PLAYS

Here are dozens of specific ideas for hands-off role-plays. Some of these might seem immediately appealing to you while others might require some research and/or planning time. Either way, you'll have a wealth of options available so you can tailor your sessions to the recipient's preferences.

Q&A ROLE-PLAYS

These ideas all involve asking questions of the recipient so he or she feels personal attention.

Application Role-Plays

- **Summary:** Application role-plays involve the other person providing information to be reviewed and potentially approved. The advantage of this type of Q&A is that the questions are mostly impersonal, and you can end the scenario with the good news of an approval.
- **Types of forms:** application forms, interview forms, request forms, registration forms, booking forms, membership forms, entry forms, sign-up forms.
- **Examples:** job application, school application, financial-aid application, loan application, scholarship application, vendor application, driver application, permit request, conference registration, camp registration, event registration, business registration, club membership, competition entry.

Feedback Role-Plays

- **Summary:** Feedback role-plays involve the other person providing information about his or her experience, perspective, or knowledge. The advantage of this type of Q&A is that the other person may feel special and valued because your questions show him or her that you care what he or she thinks.
- **Types of forms:** feedback forms, survey forms, evaluation forms.
- **Examples:** customer service evaluation, teacher evaluation, research survey, complaint form, course evaluation, satisfaction survey.

Self-Assessment Role-Plays

- **Summary:** Assessment role-plays involve the other person providing information about him- or herself as part of a self-assessment. The advantage of this type of Q&A is that the other person may feel heightened personal attention because the questions are deeper and more personal.
- **Types of forms:** assessments, questionnaires, tests, exams, quizzes.
- **Examples:** personality quiz, compatibility quiz, vocational assessment, aptitude test.

Document Role-Plays

- **Summary:** Document role-plays involve the other person providing information to simply complete a form. The advantage of this type of Q&A is that some of the forms, although not all, may be free of personal or sensitive questions.
- **Types of forms:** general documentation forms, reservation forms, order forms.
- **Examples:** motor vehicle forms, tax forms, medical history forms, consumer feedback forms, hotel reservations, car reservations, product order forms.

CONSULTATION ROLE-PLAYS

These ideas focus on role-plays in which you'll offer professional assistance or advice to the recipient.

Optometrist
Summary: Meeting with an optometrist for a vision test. This is a hands-off eye test that only focuses on the use of an eye chart

because it is done from a distance. You can use an official Snellen eye chart for your role-play or any framed picture, large book cover, or poster with words on it. Use your finger or pointer to tap on each word or letter.

Pharmacist

Summary: Meeting with a pharmacist to ask about medications. Don't use any real medications in this role-play or provide any real medication advice. Research a specific disorder and write a fake prescription on a Post-it note. Have the other person bring the note to your pharmacy counter. Fill the prescription by placing buttons or appropriately-sized candies (e.g., M&M's, Tic Tac mints) into a small cylindrical container. Incorporate a real pill-counting tray to add authentic tapping and sorting sounds. Inform the person how his or her medication will treat the disorder and counsel him or her about how to take the medication properly.

Beautician

Summary: Meeting with a beautician, cosmetologist, aesthetician, or cosmetician for a beauty consultation. Consultation can include tips and suggestions for makeup, perfume, hairstyle, hair color, shampoo selections, nail care, and skin care. Tap on bottles and containers and frequently remove lids to provide trigger sounds.

Trip Planner

Summary: Meeting with a tourist center staff person, park ranger, or hotel concierge. The role-play centers around a map and creating a trip. The map can be a highway map, hiking trail map, or a visual map for walking around a town or city. Begin by unfolding the map carefully and pressing out the creases. Use a pointer or pencil to begin outlining a path to travel. Write down stopping points or key attractions on a separate piece of paper.

Focus most of the time on tapping, tracing, and gesturing to the details of the map and the possible places to travel.

Relaxation Coach

Summary: Meeting with a relaxation coach for a guided session. The guided sessions may involve a guided meditation, guided relaxation, or guided imagery. Take on the persona of a relaxation coach and provide suggestions, gentle commands, and mental imagery to guide the other person to clear his or her mind, calm his or her thoughts, relax his or her muscles, slow his or her breathing, and visualize tranquil scenarios.

Motivational Counselor

Summary: Meeting with a motivational counselor for encouragement to achieve a goal. Goals could be related to wellness, fitness, relationships, finance, spirituality, travel, life balance, learning a new skill, attempting a new sport, studying a new language, starting a new business, or achieving any dream. This is a role-play, so you can also pretend to be an expert in a field related to the other person's goal. Provide genuine encouragement, guidance, and suggestions for the person to achieve his or her goal. If the goal is related to making a big change that may affect his or her health or safety in any way, encourage the participant to discuss the goal with a real clinician first.

Therapist

Summary: Meeting with a therapist to discuss an issue or concern. Focus on listening and trying to understand the concern, the background of the concern, and the feelings around it. Make sure the person understands that nothing you say should be a replacement for or a deterrent to actual professional advice or therapy. In fact, genuinely encouraging him or her to talk to a professional in the field of his or her concern should be included in the scenario.

Teacher

Summary: Meeting with a teacher for assistance with a topic or assignment. You can begin the scenario by stating something similar to, "I understand you are struggling to understand _____. Don't worry; it can be a difficult topic, but I will walk you through it." Have a picture of a geographic region, biological system, or historic family tree attached to a clipboard or other hard surface that allows you to create tapping sounds. Use a pointer or pencil to tap on and trace the details of the picture. Alternately, sketch out some type of visual lesson or solve mathematical problems on paper or a small whiteboard. Ideally, pick a topic you are most comfortable with and can actually teach. Sit next to the person or across from the person and explain the information carefully and patiently, but not in a condescending way.

> "In my office scene in Whisperlodge, I evoke a teacher-student relationship. Writing and performing this scene involved considering the memories of being a student and having a teacher, which is the role of the guest, and identifying the daily routines and rituals that might become nodes of nostalgia. My scene involves instruction. It involves the authority of having knowledge and transmitting it. It involves me standing up and overseeing the work of the guest, who is seated in a chair in front of me."
>
> —Andrew Hoepfner, cocreator of Whisperlodge, USA

SALES ROLE-PLAYS

The following ideas are for presentations in which you can offer information and advice about products or services.

Yard Sale

- Place an assortment of items on a table and offer them for sale. Provide real or made-up personal stories for each object.
- Be kind and flexible about the prices, of course.

Media Store

- Place your collection of music, movies, or video games on a table and offer them for sale. Introduce yourself as an employee, welcome the person to the store (make up a name), and ask if he or she is looking for anything specific. Share your genuine enthusiasm for each item.
- Most media objects will be ideal for tapping.

Beauty Product Sales

- Place a selection of perfumes, makeup, and hair care and nail care products on a table for sale. Tap on objects and frequently remove lids to provide trigger sounds.
- Remember, don't apply any makeup on the other person or touch him or her in any way if you are doing a hands-off role-play. Additionally, don't spray the perfumes in case the fumes or scents bother the other person.

Clothing and Accessories

- Fill a table with your favorite (clean) shoes, purses, jewelry, or other articles and accessories. Offer them for sale as if you were in a high-end retail store.
- You can make the prices high and then justify the costs by expressing your true enthusiasm for the items.

Cooking or Dining Products

- Place kitchen items of specific themes on a table. Items could be dishes, eating utensils, cooking utensils, cooking containers, storage containers, spices, sauces, or cooking appliances.
- Offer them for sale with demonstrations and explanations of why you value these items.
- The variety of items should offer great opportunities for tapping.

Food or Beverage Tasting

- Display foods or drinks of a similar theme on a table. Potential items include chocolates, cheeses, vegetables, fruits, and wines. Provide samples for each of you to taste. It does not need to be a large assortment; just a few items can work better because it will encourage you to take your time with each item.
- Unwrap food slowly to enhance crinkling sounds.
- Take small, delicate bites or sips frequently and talk about the flavors, the textures, and the places and times you think of when you smell or taste the item. This is an ideal scenario for those who enjoy mouth and eating sounds.

Cookbook Sales

- If you have a variety of cookbooks, then lay them out on a table to have a cookbook sale. Mark the pages of your favorite recipes and read parts of the recipes softly. For large cookbooks with colorful pictures, display the pictures to the other person while you lightly touch the items in the picture and talk about them.

- This is an ideal role-play for those who enjoy the sounds of pages turning.

Cooking or Plating Demonstrations

- Select a recipe and perform a cooking demonstration. Prepare each aspect of the recipe or prepare sections ahead of time for a simpler demonstration. If part of the preparation involves a loud noise, then try to perform that action before the scenario.
- As part of the cooking demonstration, or as its own type of role-play, demonstrate the best way to lay out the food on a plate. Delicately add sprigs, garnishes, and other details during the plating to enhance ASMR.

Catalog Sales

- Using catalogs is an easy way to do a sales role-play. If you don't have any catalogs, then just request some—companies are more than happy to send them.
- Tailor the catalog to the hobbies and interests of the other person. Consider catalogs about gardening, home decor, clothing, musical instruments, computers, sports equipment, beauty products, specialty foods, holiday decorations, skateboards, and anything else you can think of.
- Gently read descriptions and lightly touch or trace pictures with your fingertips. Catalogs tend to have thin pages, making them ideal for paper crinkling and page-turning sounds.

Magazine Sales

- With catalog sales the products are inside the catalog, but with magazine sales, the product *is* the magazine. Browse through the different sections of a magazine and explain how they contribute to its value.

- As with catalog sales, select magazines that interest the other person, lightly touch or trace pictures, and gently turn pages to enhance paper trigger sounds.

Real Estate Agent

- Real estate booklets and large brochures can be used for real estate role-plays. These booklets are free and can be found at real estate agencies or other public areas that dispense free newspapers or periodicals.
- Take on the role of a real estate agent, ask the other person what type of house he or she is looking for, and then browse through the booklet, selecting some appropriate houses.

Travel or Tourism Agent

- If you have lived in, lived near, or visited a tourist area, then you have probably seen those racks of pamphlets for popular sites and activities in that area. You can find these types of pamphlets at travel agencies, town halls, information centers on highways, hotel and motel lobbies, some family restaurants, and some convenience stores. These pamphlets can work well as part of a travel or tourism agent role-play. Ideally, try to collect pamphlets from places you have actually been to make your explanations more genuine.
- Open up each pamphlet slowly to produce paper sounds, brush your hand softly across the creases to help them stay flat, and touch and tap lightly on the pictures with your fingernails or fingertips.

Here are some additional ideas for hands-off role-plays: bedtime storytelling, caring friend/boyfriend/girlfriend, psychic reading, portrait painting, or drawing.

NEXT-LEVEL ROLE-PLAYS

Still looking for more ideas? Ready to take your role-plays to a new stratosphere? How about doing a role-play as a Jedi apprentice, a Three Mile Island accident medical examiner, a cryogenic sleep experiment researcher, a Tin Foil Hat Society member, a wounded hiker, a plague doctor, an alien android repair person, Peter Rabbit, a mall cop, Cthulhu Claus, or a pet potato caretaker. You will find all these role-plays and more in this playlist of more than 350 video ASMR role-plays (hands on and hands off) from the hypercreative Ephemeral Rift: www.youtube.com/playlist?list=PLvYncOsqMfxyAtQ0bkM6aW7wuQ43K_uN5.

BIBLIOGRAPHY

"5 Things You Should Know about Stress." National Institute of Mental Health. Accessed March 8, 2018. www.nimh.nih.gov/health/publications/stress/index.shtml.

Anderzén-Carlsson, A., Lamy, Z.C., and Eriksson, M. (2014). "Parental Experiences of Providing Skin-to-Skin Care to Their Newborn Infant—Part 1: A Qualitative Systematic Review." *International Journal of Qualitative Studies on Health and Well-Being* 9: 1–22.

"Any Anxiety Disorder." National Institute of Mental Health. Last modified November 2017. www.nimh.nih.gov/health/statistics/prevalence/any-anxiety-disorder-among-adults.shtml.

Apprich, F. (2016). "The Benefits of ASMR in Education." *IOSR Journal of Research & Method in Education* 6(5): 113–18.

Barratt, E.L., and Davis, N.J. (2015). "Autonomous Sensory Meridian Response (ASMR): A Flow-Like Mental State." *PeerJ* 3:e851.

Barratt, E.L., Spence, C., and Davis, N.J. (2017). "Sensory Determinants of the Autonomous Sensory Meridian Response (ASMR): Understanding the Triggers." *PeerJ* 5:e3846.

"Brain Basics: Understanding Sleep." National Institute of Neurological Disorders and Stroke. Last modified May 22, 2017. www.ninds.nih.gov/Disorders/Patient-Caregiver-Education/Understanding-Sleep.

Coryell, W., and Winokur, G. "Overview of Mood Disorders." Merck Manual. Last modified May 2018. www.merckmanuals.com/professional/psychiatric-disorders/mood-disorders/overview-of-mood-disorders.

"Depression." National Institute of Mental Health. Last modified February 2018. www.nimh.nih.gov/health/topics/depression/index.shtml.

Dubuc, B. "Chronobiology." McGill University. Accessed March 8, 2018. http://thebrain.mcgill.ca/flash/i/i_11/i_11_p/i_11_p_hor/i_11_p_hor.html.

Fredborg, B.K., Clark, J., and Smith, S.D. (2017). "An Examination of Personality Traits Associated with Autonomous Sensory Meridian Response (ASMR)." *Frontiers in Psychology* 8: 247.

Inagaki, T.K., Ray, L.A., Irwin, M.R., Way, B.M., and Eisenberger, N.I. (2016). "Opioids and Social Bonding: Naltrexone Reduces Feelings of Social Connection." *Social Cognitive and Affective Neuroscience* 11(5): 728–35.

Janik McErlean, A.B., and Banissy, M.J. (2017). "Assessing Individual Variation in Personality and Empathy Traits in Self-Reported Autonomous Sensory Meridian Response." *Multisensory Research* 30(6): 601–13.

Kirsch, P. (2015). "Oxytocin in the Socioemotional Brain: Implications for Psychiatric Disorders." *Dialogues in Clinical Neuroscience* 17(4): 463–76.

Parashar, P., Samuel, A.J., Bansal, A., and Aranka, V.P. (2016). "Yakson Touch As a Part of Early Intervention in the Neonatal Intensive Care Unit: A Systematic Narrative Review." *Indian Journal of Critical Care Medicine* 20(6): 349–52.

"Relaxation Techniques for Health." National Center for Complementary and Integrative Health. Last modified April 20, 2017. https://nccih.nih.gov/health/stress/relaxation.htm.

Richard, C.A.H. "Interview with Jennifer Allen, the Woman Who Coined the Term, 'Autonomous Sensory Meridian Response' (ASMR)." ASMR University. May 17, 2016. https://asmruniversity.com/2016/05/17/jennifer-allen-interview-coined-asmr/.

Richard, C.A.H. "Voices of ASMR: A Collection of ASMR Experiences." ASMR University. Accessed March 8, 2018. https://asmruniversity.com/voices-of-asmr/.

Richard, C.A.H., Burnett, K., and Allen, J. "ASMR Research Project." ASMR University. Accessed March 8, 2018. https://asmruniversity.com/asmr-survey/.

Sippel, L.M., Allington, C.E., Pietrzak, R.H., Harpaz-Rotem, I., Mayes, L.C., and Olff, M. (2017). "Oxytocin and Stress-Related Disorders: Neurobiological Mechanisms and Treatment Opportunities." *Chronic Stress (Thousand Oaks)* 1: 1–24.

"Sleep Disorders." Mayo Clinic. Last modified September 14, 2016. www.mayoclinic.org/diseases-conditions/sleep-disorders/symptoms-causes/syc-20354018.

Smith, S.D., Fredborg, B.K., and Kornelsen, J. (2017). "An Examination of the Default Mode Network in Individuals with Autonomous Sensory Meridian Response (ASMR)." *Social Neuroscience* 12(4): 361–65.

Suvilehto, J.T., Glerean, E., Dunbar, R.I.M., Hari, R., and Nummenmaa, L. (2015). "Topography of Social Touching Depends on Emotional Bonds Between Humans." *Proceedings of the National Academy of Sciences of the United States of America* 112(45): 13,811–16.

Taylor, J.H., Mustoe, A.C., Hochfelder, B., and French, J.A. (2015). "Reunion Behavior after Social Separation Is Associated with Enhanced HPA Recovery in Young Marmoset Monkeys." *Psychoneuroendocrinology* 57: 93–101.

APPENDIX A: ASMR TRIGGER MENU

This list of triggers is a good way to ask recipients what type of triggers to include and exclude from ASMR sessions. They can check their preferences and return the form to you. Please visit https://asmruniversity.com/brain-tingles-forms/ to download a copy of this form.

Recipient's Name: _____

TYPE OF TRIGGER	Include	Exclude	Not Sure; Will Try
Velvety Voices			
Speaking Style			
Gentle voice			
Soft whisper			
Trigger Toolbox			
Trigger words			
Unintelligible speaking			
Foreign languages			
Rambling			
Reading			
Guided sessions			
Soothing Sounds			
Presentation			
In-front view			
Ear to ear			
Behind head			

TYPE OF TRIGGER	Include	Exclude	Not Sure; Will Try
Trigger Toolbox			
Crinkling sounds			
Tapping sounds			
Scratching sounds			
Sticking sounds			
Mouth sounds			
Squishing sounds			
Action sounds			
Item sounds			
Feathery Fingers			
Trigger Toolbox			
Hair			
Scalp			
Face			
Shoulders			
Back			
Arms			
Hands			
Legs			
Tingly Tools			
Trigger Toolbox			
Scalp massagers			
Hairbrushes, combs, and picks			
Makeup brushes and paintbrushes			
Fuzzy and smooth fabrics			

TYPE OF TRIGGER	Include	Exclude	Not Sure; Will Try
Scratching tools			
Feathers and cat toys			
Tranquil Treasures			
Presentation			
Visible item			
Mystery package			
Mystery box			
Unboxing			
Haul			
Collection			
Trigger Toolbox			
Common collectibles			
Media and accessories			
Print items			
Cosmetics			
Grooming items			
Clothing and accessories			
Home items			
Food items			
Assuaging Activities			
Presentation			
With narration			
Without narration			
Trigger Toolbox			
Painting			
Drawing and writing			

TYPE OF TRIGGER	Include	Exclude	Not Sure; Will Try
Coloring			
Solving puzzles			
Tabletop game tutorials			
Magic tricks			
Reading or browsing			
Device demonstrations			
Video game demonstrations			
Software demonstrations			
Makeup application			
Hand care			
Hair care			
Hands-On Role-Plays			
Trigger Toolbox—Clinical Role-Plays			
Physical exam			
Cranial nerve exam			
Ear exam			
Ear cleaning			
Eye exam			
Head lice exam			
Cranial phrenology exam			
Hand exam			
Skin exam			
Trigger Toolbox—Beauty-Care Role-Plays			
Haircuts and trims with scissors			
Haircuts and shaves with clippers			

TYPE OF TRIGGER	Include	Exclude	Not Sure; Will Try
Face and neck shave			
Hairstyling			
Makeup applications			
Hand and nail care			
Tattoo applications			
Hands-Off Role-Plays			
Trigger Toolbox—Q&A Role-Plays			
Applications			
Feedback			
Self-assessments			
Documents			
Trigger Toolbox—Consultation Role-Plays			
Optometrist			
Pharmacist			
Beautician			
Relaxation coach			
Motivational counselor			
Therapist			
Teacher			
Trigger Toolbox—Sales and Demonstration Role-Plays			
Yard sale			
Media store			
Beauty product sale			
Clothing and accessories sale			
Cooking or dining products			

TYPE OF TRIGGER	Include	Exclude	Not Sure; Will Try
Food or beverage tasting			
Cookbook sale			
Cooking or plating demonstration			
Catalog sale			
Magazine sale			
Real estate agent			
Travel or tourism agent			

APPENDIX B:
ASMR PERSONALIZATION FORM

This form covers consents, preferences, and allergies. Discuss this form with the recipient to help every session be a comfortable and safe experience. Complete this form prior to the first session, then consult it before each future session with this participant and update it as necessary as preferences change. Please visit https://asmruniversity.com/brain-tingles-forms/ to download a copy of this form.

Recipient's Name: _____

Consents

Okay to be touched directly (with fingers and hands)? Yes/No

Okay to be touched indirectly (with items and objects)? Yes/No

Okay to sit closely in his or her personal space? Yes/No

If touching is allowed, select a safe word or action that can be used anytime that a touch feels uncomfortable in any way.

Safe word: _____

Safe action: _____

If touching is allowed, select allowable areas:

Head: Yes/No

Notes: _____

_____

_____

Neck: Yes/No

Notes: _____

_____

_____

Shoulders/Back: Yes/No

Notes: _____

_____

_____

Arms: Yes/No

Notes: _____

_____

_____

Hands: Yes/No

Notes: _____

_____

_____

Lower Legs: Yes/No

Notes: _____

_____

_____

Feet: Yes/No

Notes: _____

_____

_____

Trigger Preferences

Consult the ASMR Trigger Menu or the "Trigger Toolbox" section of each chapter for suggestions.

Chapter 3: Velvety Voices

- Toolbox favorites: _____
- Technique preferences: _____

Chapter 4: Soothing Sounds

- Toolbox favorites: _____
- Technique preferences: _____

Chapter 5: Feathery Fingers

- Toolbox favorites: _____
- Technique preferences: _____

Chapter 6: Tingly Tools

- Toolbox favorites: _____
- Technique preferences: _____

Chapter 7: Tranquil Treasures

- Toolbox favorites: _____

- Technique preferences: _____

Chapter 8: Assuaging Activities

- Toolbox favorites: _____

- Technique preferences: _____

Chapter 9: Hands-On Role-Plays

- Toolbox favorites: _____

- Technique preferences: _____

Chapter 10: Hands-Off Role-Plays

- Toolbox favorites: _____

- Technique preferences: _____

Known Allergies and Sensitivities

Latex allergy? Yes/No

Notes: _____

_____

Animal allergy? Yes/No

Notes: _____

_____

Metal allergy? Yes/No

Notes: _____

_____

Fragrance sensitivity? Yes/No

Notes: _____

_____

Other allergy or sensitivity? Yes/No

Notes: _____

_____

ADDITIONAL IMPORTANT INFORMATION

_____

_____

_____

_____

_____

_____

_____

_____

_____

_____

APPENDIX C: ASMR SESSION PLAN

Use this form to map out your trigger plan for each session. Spending a few minutes ahead of time to figure out what you'll do and for how long will eliminate time spent fumbling for tools and awkward spaces between triggers. Create a new and different plan for each future session to provide variety for the recipient. Please visit https://asmruniversity.com/brain-tingles-forms/ to download a copy of this form.

Recipient's Name: _____ Date: _____

Pre-Session

- Review the recipient's ASMR Personalization Form for his or her preferences and potential allergies.
- If the recipient prefers, review this session plan with him or her prior to starting the session, then revise accordingly.

Session Phases

Preparation Phase: Relaxation Exercise
(about 5 minutes)

- Exercise: _____

_____

_____

_____

Entry Phase: Single Triggers
(about 10 minutes total)

- Trigger: _____

_____

_____

- Trigger: _____

_____

_____

- Trigger: _____

_____

_____

Immersion Phase: Combination Triggers
(about 15–30 minutes total)

- Triggers: _____

_____

_____

- Triggers: _____

_____

_____

- Triggers: _____

_____

_____

Return Phase: Single Triggers
(about 10 minutes total)

- Trigger: _____

  _____

  _____

- Trigger: _____

  _____

  _____

- Trigger: _____

  _____

  _____

Landing Phase: Quiet
(about 5 minutes)

- Remain quiet with eyes closed and mind cleared.

Post-Session

- Discuss anything that the person particularly liked or did not like.
- Update the recipient's ASMR Personalization Form accordingly.

INDEX

A

Allen, Jennifer, 21–22
Allergies, 127–28
Allergies form, 224–29
Anxiety, reducing, 30–32
ASMR (Autonomous Sensory Meridian Response). *See also* Brain tingles
allergies form, 224–29
benefits of, 7–10, 29–34
biological origins of, 24–28
classes on, 38
consent form, 224–29
in daily life, 29–52
defining, 15
expectations of, 41–42
experiencing, 7–10, 15–16, 42
history of, 19–24
partner ASMR, 36–40, 48–53, 57–58, 127
personalization form, 224–29
physical sensations of, 15–16, 42
popularity of, 22–24
preferences for, 49–51
preferences form, 224–29
preparing for, 33–52
psychological sensations of, 16
scheduling sessions for, 40–47
self-stimulation of, 34–36
sensations of, 15–16, 42
sensitivities form, 224–29
session plan, 50–51, 230–32
solitary ASMR, 34–36
stimulation of, 7–10, 34–36
tools for, 53–172
trigger menu form, 218–23
trigger preferences form, 224–29
triggers of, 10–11, 15–29
understanding, 7–8, 13–32
videos featuring, 7, 9–10, 16, 18, 20–24, 32–35, 45–52, 69, 95–96, 116, 140, 147, 174, 178–89, 195–200
ASMR *Facebook* groups, 20–23, 74
Assuaging activities
benefits of, 153–72
browsing, 166–67
coloring, 163
drawing, 162–63
electronic devices, 167–68
focus on, 157–58
foundations of, 153–55
games, 164–65
hair care, 171
hand care, 170
ideas for, 156–72
magic tricks, 165
makeup application, 169–70
narrating, 159–61
painting, 162
performing, 157–58
puzzles, 164
reading, 166–67
role-plays and, 172, 192
safety precautions with, 156
selecting, 156–57
software, 168–69
trigger tips for, 156–61
trigger toolbox for, 161–72
video games, 168
watching, 153–70
writing, 162–63
Audio triggers, 17. *See also* Triggers

B

Beauty-care role-plays. *See also* Role-plays
description of, 181, 183–84
electric clippers and, 190
face shaves, 190–91
haircuts, 189–90

L

Lauw, Melinda, 8, 65, 108, 129, 158, 179

M

Marketing messages, 9, 24
Massage, 43, 113, 116, 131–32
"Medicine touch," 106
Melatonin, 28, 46
Mood, improving, 32
Morren, Jolien, 71, 107

N

Newborns, 105–6. *See also* Infants
Noise masking, 82. *See also* Soothing sounds

O

Observation triggers, 18–19. *See also* Triggers
Oxytocin, 25–28, 47, 105

P

Partner ASMR, 36–40, 48–53, 57–58, 127
Personalization form, 224–29
Physical sensations, 15–16, 42
Picasso, Pablo, 158
Pollock, Jackson, 158
Preferences, discussing, 49–51
Preferences form, 224–29
Preparation for ASMR, 33–52
Props
    for beauty-care role-plays, 189–93
    for clinical role-plays, 182–89
    clipboards, 182–84, 197
    costumes, 173–75, 182, 192
    for hands-off role-plays, 197–98

for hands-on role-plays, 173–75, 182–93
    name badges, 197–98
    pointers, 196, 198
Psychological sensations, 16

Q

Q&A role-plays
    application role-plays, 205
    description of, 201–2
    document role-plays, 206
    feedback role-plays, 205
    self-assessment role-plays, 206
    types of, 205–6

R

Reading
    bedtime stories, 73–75
    fables, 75
    fiction, 75
    instructions, 77–78
    lists, 76–77
    nonfiction, 77–78
    plays, 76
    poems, 76
    recipes, 77
    short stories, 75
    song lyrics, 76
    topics for, 75–78
    voices for, 73–74
Relaxation, 7–10, 29–30
Relaxing role-plays, 173–91, 197–208. *See also* Role-plays
Richard, Craig, 8
Riggs, Bobby, 191
Role-plays
    action plan for, 174–75
    assuaging activities and, 172, 192
    beauty-care role-plays, 181, 183–84, 189–93
    clinical role-plays, 180–89
    consent for, 180

Trigger preferences form, 224–29
Triggers
    audio triggers, 17
    description of, 10–11, 15–29
    explanation of, 17–19
    foreign languages, 70–72
    forms for, 218–29
    length of time per, 50–51
    observation triggers, 18–19
    scenario triggers, 19
    touch triggers, 17–18, 49–50,
        108–22
    trigger words, 67–69
    types of, 17–19, 49–50, 53
    unintelligible speaking, 69–70
    for velvety voices, 55–79
Troubleshooting issues, 51–52

V

Velvety voices
    benefits of, 55–79
    breath for sessions, 56, 64–67, 78
    considerations for, 55–79
    ear-to-ear sounds, 61–62, 68, 79,
        85–87
    eye contact and, 60
    foreign languages, 70–72
    foundations of, 55
    guided sessions for, 78–79
    intentions for, 56–57
    pace for, 58–59
    pitch for, 59–60
    rambling, 72–73
    reading, 73–74
    seating for sessions, 62
    silence for sessions, 64
    tone for, 57–58
    trigger tips for, 55–79
    trigger toolbox for, 67–79
    trigger words for, 67–69
    unintelligible speaking, 69–70
    viewing materials for, 63–64
    volume for, 57, 61
    water for sessions, 62–63

whispering, 64–67, 69–70
Videos
    on ASMR, 7, 9–10, 16, 18, 20–24,
        32–35, 45–52, 69, 95–96, 116,
        140, 147, 174, 178–89, 195–200
    of Bob Ross painting, 9–10, 18, 92,
        154–55, 160
    on brain tingles, 9–10
    making, 52
    for role-plays, 174, 178–89, 193,
        195–200, 210, 214
    whisper videos, 20–21, 65
Volume of voice, 57, 61, 70, 81–84,
    160. *See also* Soothing sounds;
    Velvety voices

W

Well-being, improving, 32
Whispers
    broken whisper, 66
    evil whisper, 66–67
    harsh whisper, 66
    inaudible whisper, 69–70
    for sessions, 64–67
    tips for, 64–67
Whisper videos, 20–21, 65

Y

Yakson, 106
YouTube videos, 7, 9–10, 18, 20–24,
    95–96, 116, 147. *See also* Videos